PENGUIN BOOKS

WAKE UP TO YOUR DREAMS

Joan Hanger is an authority throughout Australasia on dream analysis. She has completed studies at the C.G. Jung Institute in Zurich, Switzerland, to which she returns frequently to supplement her knowledge. Joan makes regular national television appearances and writes feature articles for a number of magazines. She is also the author of *In Your Dreams*.

WAKE UP TO YOUR DREAMS

JOAN HANGER

with Catherine Hanger

PENGUIN BOOKS

Penguin Books India (P) Ltd., 11 Community Centre, Panchsheel Park,
New Delhi 110017, India
Penguin Books Ltd., 80 Strand, London WC2R ORL, UK
Penguin Putnam Inc., 375 Hudson Street, New York, NY 10014, USA
Penguin Books Australia Ltd. Ringwood, Victoria, Australia
Penguin Books Canada Ltd., 10 Alcorn Avenue, Suite 300, Toronto, Ontario, M4V 3B2, Canada
Penguin Books (NZ) Ltd., Cnr Rosedale & Airborne Roads, Albany, Auckland, New Zealand

First published by Penguin Books Australia Ltd 1997
First published in India by Penguin Books India 2001

10 9 8 7 6 5 4 3 2 1

Typeset in AGaramond by S.R. Enterprises, New Delhi
Printed at Chaman Offset Printers, New Delhi

Contents

Introduction

The reason you are reading this book is that you dream. Everyone does. We have all heard of history's giants who have been led by powerful visions, but the fact is that perfectly ordinary people are capable of having extraordinary dreams. The question is, what do we do with them? We can simply dismiss them as meaningless bubbles percolating from minds dissolved by sleep. But that is not why you are reading this book. Most likely, you are reading this book because you suspect that your dreams — confused pictures

Dreams are the touchstones of our characters.

– HENRY DAVID THOREAU

imperfectly remembered — are somehow profoundly connected with your state of mind and your deepest sense of being.

You're right. Your dreams are messages from you to your Self. Read on.

Everyone dreams, but not everyone remembers their dreams. I have often spoken to people who claim that they do not dream, only to have them remember fragments of dreams as we converse. Dreams are hard to grasp because they are related to our unconscious psyche, which expresses itself in a different way to our conscious thoughts. Dreams are formulations of our unconscious, feeding elusive but powerful images to the waking mind across the tenuous bridge of memory. But the mind is a whole entity, with different ways of expressing different things. Because people in Western societies overrate the intellect and the material world, the challenge is to integrate the conscious and the unconscious.

Memory is the conundrum. This book explores the ways in which you can heighten the recall of your dreams, as well as interpret them for yourself to enrich your life.

1
Why dream?

THE ROLE OF MEMORY

One of the most extraordinary facts about dreams is that they may utilise memories of events and people that the dreamer has long forgotten. It seems that we truly forget very little, and that everything in the vast storehouse of memory, which is tucked away somewhere in the unconscious mind, is available for the purposes of the imaginative construction of our dreams. So we may include in our dreams snippets from childhood, old conversations, and places and objects that have nothing to do with our present-day circumstances. They may seem to be insignificant, but each element of the dream exists for a reason. Usually the

There seems something more speakingly incomprehensible in the powers, the failures, the inequalities of memory, than in any other of our intelligences.

– JANE AUSTEN, *MANSFIELD PARK*

presence of these memories indicates that they have some pertinent tie, symbolically, to a current situation, the situation that is being figured out in the dream.

While our dreams may have 'remembered' what our conscious thoughts do not, dreams themselves are not easily recalled. It appears that in REM sleep — the phase of sleep when we dream most vividly — the brain cells that secrete the chemicals needed to stimulate memory shut down or operate sluggishly. This is one of the reasons why it is so often difficult to remember dreams; the other reason is simply cognitive. (See below for a further explanation of REM sleep.)

When we are awake the conscious mind is paramount. We are self-aware. We can exercise critical judgment and our decisions and opinions are formed by logic, which is necessarily a linear structure. But when we are asleep all these faculties are suspended, so that when we dream we are without the contemplative adjuncts to waking thought; we are entirely involved in the dream. (A notable exception is lucid dreaming, which is best described as the realisation in the dream that we are dreaming. This subject is treated in more depth later.) We accept the dream landscape and all its characters as real, and our emotions respond accordingly. And finally, without the rudders of empirical logic and critical distance, we 'dream think' in metaphor and symbol.

These are perfectly valid ways of processing information, and in fact happen constantly, even in the waking state. It is just that this form of comprehending is usually masked by the logic of the conscious mind.

THE NATURE OF SLEEP

Sleep is not a uniform state. We descend through various strata to deep sleep, and drift back up again to almost waking many times per night. It has been suggested that we 'wake' up to fifteen times in a night, but forget these events as we drift deeper again.

Sleep is apparently necessary for a balanced life. While many people do not seem to need the standard adult quota of 8 hours, others need far more; there is no real uniformity. However, one fact that was established early in the history of sleep research was this: when people are kept awake for long periods they can suffer from extreme irritability, poor concentration, and even hallucinations and temporary psychosis.

To sleep: perchance to dream ...

–WILLIAM SHAKESPEARE, *HAMLET*

As our comprehension of the stages of sleep became more sophisticated, the phenomenon of REM sleep was discovered. This phase of sleep holds the key to the physiological features of dreams. It was discovered that it was REM deprivation that led to the symptoms of irritability, poor concentration and so on, described above. And it was discovered that most dreams occur during REM phases of sleep, which occur about four and up to seven times per night. It may well be that the physiological need to sleep is intimately connected to the psychological need to dream.

REM is an acronym for Rapid Eye Movement, which is what researchers observed their sleeping subjects doing during these phases — under closed eyelids, of course! Observation of the sleeping state has been further enhanced by laboratory techniques involving the attachment of electroencephalographs, which measure the electrical activity of the brain during sleep. Apart from a short (about 1 hour) phase of very deep sleep when brain waves diminish considerably, the brain's activity when a person is asleep is almost as pronounced as when they are awake.

Various stages and corresponding dream activities have been clearly identified. Sleep is made up of repetitive phases, each containing four distinct levels. Each one of these phases with its four levels I call a sleep undulation. The onset of sleep is marked by short visions and images called *hypnagogic dreams*. After this, the sleeper drops through four levels to deep sleep, before floating slowly up through the shallows into the first occurrence of REM sleep. The sleeper then drops again, but rarely to quite as deep a level as in the first undulation. As the sleeper rises each time, the period of REM sleep becomes longer. The final REM period can last as long as 40 minutes.

Dreams can occur at all levels, but dreams occurring during REM sleep are the most vivid. Physiological changes, apart from eye movement, are also apparent. Men usually have an erection, and women (less obviously) show increased flow of blood to the vagina. The heart rate speeds up, breathing is erratic and muscles twitch. We have all seen dogs chasing cats in their sleep!

However, with all this evidence of movement, there is another feature of REM sleep that the body, in its wisdom, ensures is in place. This is the paralysis of the muscles. Sleepwalking and talking occur in other levels, not in REM sleep. Rather ironically, in the level where dreams are the most vivid, our bodies are prevented from moving. There is wide conjecture that this may be why we often dream of being unable to move away from a terrifying pursuer, and why some people have the frightening experience of feeling paralysed on awakening.

One dreamer related to me a dream she had been experiencing where she realised she could not move because she was paralysed. In the dream, she also heard the telephone ringing — evidence that her sleep was quite shallow. The feeling terrified her, and remained very vivid as she woke, but she was reassured to know that this sort of dream on awakening is quite common. It is important to note also that the circumstances of the woman's life were quite stressful: she was experiencing marital problems at the time.This added stress and feeling in real life of being frustrated and unable to move on would have contributed to the strength of the symbol.

Because REM sleep is relatively shallow, it is the time when we are most likely to wake if our dreams are particularly striking. People woken deliberately during REM sleep have no trouble describing their dreams.

Another interesting feature of this level of sleep is that any small physical change that is not enough to wake the sleeper will be effortlessly introduced into the dream in some imaginative form. An alarm clock may be incorporated as a church bell; a breeze over skin may be experienced in the dream as a feeling of nakedness or a gale-force wind. This is probably because the effect of small stimuli is heightened in the absence of other physical distractions.

THE SYMBOLIC NATURE OF DREAMS

Symbols are pictorial representations of ideas, states, feelings or even beings that have a wider connotation than their obvious meaning. They are formed spontaneously, because they are largely unconscious. All symbols — whether created in the crucible of our sleeping minds or the crucible of the artist's inspiration — are vehicles. They carry meaning that is otherwise inexpressible. They are 'numinous'. This lovely word, often used by Carl Gustav Jung, means that they are transcendent, connecting us with something that is more than ourselves. The meaning of symbols is most adequately grasped instinctively. In trying to anatomise a symbol with pure logic, we often miss the most definitive — numinous — bit of it.

As a plant produces its flower so the psyche creates its symbols.

– C.G. JUNG, *MAN AND HIS SYMBOLS*

The language of dreams is symbolic, so it is difficult to understand. A person's dreams express all their ideas, feelings and situations in a series of images that are imbued with the personal significance of the dreamer. Some of these images achieve the status of archetypes. These are symbols that have a meaning to all humanity and appear across cultures and eras in the same form. (Archetypes are discussed in greater depth in chapter three.) It is most important to note, however, that each person's dream life is unique. While many themes and symbols appear frequently, they mean nothing if divorced from the context of the dream in which they occur. Consequently, the best person to analyse your dreams is you.

But surely the demands of our conscious life are enough, so why should we remember, let alone analyse, our dreams? The answer is that dreams are evidence of the mind rebalancing itself. They convey to us our deepest feelings and instincts. Each of the experiences we have in our waking lives carries an unconscious component and some of these components have a strong psychic charge. So we re-vision in our dreams what it is we need to process, what it is we have repressed, and what it is we need to understand about our own motivations and drives. But we revise these things in dream language – in symbols – which we may have the devil of a time trying to comprehend. Remember: it is you who creates the images for yourself. At some level you know what they mean because your mind has formed them.

In our conscious world, we perceive through our five senses, and we filter these perceptions through the faculty of reason. But the mind works on many levels, and the sense-reason-consciousness triad is only one of them. Beyond this fragile layer there is the Whole Mind, which perceives life in a different way, if it 'perceives' at all. This part of our psyche is connected with the greater stream of life that is organic, animalistic, primitive. Jung observed that 'what we call civilised consciousness has steadily separated itself from the basic instincts. But these instincts have not disappeared. They have merely lost their contact with our consciousness and are thus forced to assert themselves in an indirect fashion. This may be by means of physical symptoms in the case of a neurosis, or by means of incidents of various kinds, like unaccountable moods, unexpected forgetfulness, or mistakes in speech' (1978, p. 72).

Or, of course, they may assert themselves in dreams.

We applaud ourselves on our cleverness but are helpless in the face of our instinctive urges. All that the rational person can do is compartmentalise doggedly, to keep the conscious, outer life separate from the uncontrollable, irrational, underdeveloped and unacknowledged inner life. We don't have to look further than the media to see the often extreme consequences of such dissociation in acts of violent aggression or self-abuse. Sometimes this sense of dissociation is manifested in chronic feelings of loneliness, discontent, or a nameless dread.

No wonder we have bad dreams, because dreams, produced through the numinous symbolising faculty of our psyche, put us back in touch with ourselves. Dream symbols are produced spontaneously *by ourselves, for ourselves,* to convey special messages about the real state of affairs in the internal kingdom. We ignore them at our peril!

Dreams are not always dire warnings, of course. Most of us are not critically cut off (most certainly not those of you who are reading this and are open to new ideas!), so our dreams may indicate readjustments, feed us with information on our intuitions about situations in which we find ourselves, indicate important life passages, or identify our real feelings about the people around us. They may even have a predictive function (see chapter five).

Essentially, dreams put us in touch with our own imaginations, which in turn create our dreams. Imagination allows us to inject dynamism into our lives. Imagination gives us the courage to change, to grow. It is the fount of desire, which is the fount of intent and achievement. Our dreams keep tabs on us. They let us know when we are positive, or ambivalent, or struggling. They resonate with the concerns of our everyday lives, and offer us curious, fantastical visions that complement our existence. Dreams work on the same principle as many works of art, where familiar images, situations and people are infused with symbolic meaning so that they are at once recognisable and strange.

DREAM PHILOSOPHY THROUGH HISTORY

In recent history, dreams were the key to the 'discovery' of the unconscious and the birth of psychoanalysis. Sigmund Freud's seminal work *The Interpretation of Dreams,* first published in 1899, was the first attempt to link dreams with psychological disorders. He noticed that neurotic symptoms and dreams were equally symbolic. In the neurotic patient, anxiety manifested itself in certain physical symptoms — things like an inability to speak in front of people, an obsession with hand-washing, impotence; in dreams, the same sort of anxieties were expressed symbolically in images. Freud used dreams as the basis for the analysis of the unconscious problems of the patient. Carl Gustav Jung, the greatest and most profound interpreter of dreams, studied with Freud and took the latter's findings many steps further.

Real are the dreams of Gods ...

– JOHN KEATS, *LAMIA*

Of course, the unconscious has always existed. There are many people, including myself, who have examined our Judeo-

Christian myth of Creation — Adam and Eve in the Garden of Eden — and found there a story of Man's Fall into Consciousness. Like most tales of this symbolic nature, there are resonances that radiate in all directions; but, essentially, the story depicts the transition from wholeness to fragmentation in the symbol of an apple eaten from the Tree of Knowledge.

We are told by anthropologists that when the unconscious impulses of primitive

man became too strident, he suffered a derangement which dissociated him from his environment and was commonly termed a 'loss of soul'. He lost his identity with his tribe, his totems, his culture. When modern man 'loses his soul', it usually takes the form of a split-off, or compartmentalisation, of the troubling aspects of the unconscious from the conscious. Hence, neuroses and psychoses and recurring nightmares may result. The unconscious is troubling. It behaves according to impulses that cannot be controlled and insists on breaking through our fragile, conscious layer in various forms, including dreams.

Primitive humans developed self-awareness over centuries of evolution. As their brains grew in sophistication, *homo sapiens* discovered the heady possibilities of the intellect. They made weapons, fire, houses, clothes, and all the paraphernalia that distinguished them and protected them from Nature. They learnt to use Nature for their advancement. But their instinctive responses to the rhythms and requirements of their environment still dominated their existence.

Though aware of their separateness, *homo sapiens* identified and projected. They saw beings in trees and rocks; howled out their fear in rituals where demons were personified with frightening animalistic masks and then destroyed; empowered themselves in ceremonial association with totemic creatures with whom they cohabited in the environment. They made myths and art, both of which were bridges between the physical world and the world of abstraction and dream.

Dreams were seen as messages from tribal divinities or from the other world — the world beyond death. Often they were presumed to be premonitory, and were interpreted as such. Magic personages — shamans — were those who had significant dreams and could use dream power to direct, interpret and heal. Dreams were intrinsic in structure and content to man's understanding of his context. They were windows through which he could comprehend — and project — meaning.

This view, in essence, continued on through the archaic and classical periods of history. In the Greek and Roman civilisations, for example, dreams were still thought to be introjected into the dreamer by some other agency that was more or less divine (although Aristotle undertook a purely psychological study of dreams and felt they were indicative of man's connection to nature and himself). The major point of contention was how to discern important dreams from unimportant dreams, and how to interpret those worth interpreting. Artemidorus of Daldis, in his exhaustive work *Oneirocritica* (study of dreams), sensibly classified dreams into two categories: those concerned with the past or present events with no future significance (the common and non-recurring nightmare was one of these); and those concerned with determining the future. These included dreams with a direct prophesying purpose, dreams previsioning a future event, and dreams with a significant symbolic component which required elucidation and interpretation.

From this time on, the changing relationship of humans to gods or God tended to define attitudes to dreams. The Jewish mystical teachings enshrined in the thirteenth-century Kabbalist text, the *Zohar* (Book of Splendour), explain that dreams are both messages from God and reflections of our psyches, and thus an avenue for self-exploration. The *Zohar* states that 'a dream not remembered might as well not have been dreamed, and therefore a dream forgotten and gone from mind is never fulfilled'. Furthermore, it points out that our minds work in sleep by means of symbols. Kabbalists advised both that a dream should be told, or unburdened, and the symbology discussed, and that the dreamer must be very careful about relating the dream to just anyone, because the listener can distort the interpretation. When a dream was particularly troubling, Rabbinical leaders advised a 'dreamfast' — a period of fasting and self-reflective meditation. It was felt that a dream of foreboding represented a clear warning, but not an irrevocable premonition, and that reflection could rebalance the psyche and address the causes of anxiety giving rise to the dream.

Kabbalists also believed that dreams heralded illness, and could be used therapeutically by meditating on a problem before sleep and formally asking the dreaming mind to convey a message. This method, known to Jewish Kabbalists for centuries, is known today as dream incubation.

Other religious systems have placed great importance on the function of dreaming. The Nineveh tablets, found in the tomb of an Assyrian king of the seventh century BC, contain dream formulas based on the meaning of symbols.

Throughout the Old Testament there are references to the voice of God being revealed to people through dreams.

Throughout early Christian tradition, dreams were associated with the voice of God, but later, as the church became stronger and more autocratic, dreams were associated with witchcraft and demonic influences. The voice of God was not allowed to speak through the individual, only his church. Moreover, dreams, with all their ability to conjure alarming, uncontrolled and often blatantly irreligious images, were frowned upon.

Most of the Koran was dictated to Mohammed in a dream. Islamic dream tradition made a strong distinction between divine and false dreams, and warned against false prophets. Mohammed interpreted the dreams of his disciples each morning after prayer.

Eastern religious traditions, which embrace transcendence as the aim and structure of their mythology, blur the distinction between psychic states. Dreams are seen as just another way the psyche experiences itself. They are allied to meditation and death, and the space between death and reincarnation, called, in Buddhist belief, the Bardo. The great Taoist philosopher, Chuang-tzu, wrote around 350 BC, 'Once upon a time I, Chuang-tzu, dreamed I was a butterfly. I was conscious only of following my fancies as a butterfly and was unconscious of my individuality ... Now I do not know whether I was a man dreaming I was a butterfly, or whether I am a butterfly now dreaming I am a man'.

FREUD AND JUNG

Back in the rationalist West at the end of the nineteenth century, theories of the mind were proliferating. In 1899, Sigmund Freud proposed his revolutionary theory of the unconscious. He tied the dream firmly to the individual dreaming mind, replete with all its battles between rationalism and primitive intuition, as well as its unique psychological history that would determine the dreams it had, and why. God was removed from the chain of causality.

Freud postulated that the dream is a psychic creation that is capable of being interpreted in relation to man's unconscious desires, repressions and anxieties. He undertook careful study on the characteristics of dreams (see chapter two), and theorised that all dreams were at some level wish fulfilments. He regarded the dream images as 'manifest content' that screened the dream thoughts, which he called 'latent content'. For Freud, the images of the manifest content were confusing,

... [T]he dreamer and his dream are the same ... the powers personified in a dream are those that move the world.

—JOSEPH CAMPBELL

elusive and often troubling. One of the reasons for this is that they conceal the latent wish, which is not allowed to be directly expressed. So, to identify the repressed wish (or more generally, the complex, which may be a full-blown neurosis in some cases), Freud had his patients free-associate (to follow a train of thought suggested spontaneously by an image, word, or figure of speech) around the images of the dream to arrive at the latent content. From here, the dream could truly be interpreted and the unconscious problems identified and treated.

Jung expanded on Freud's findings, and made a life-long study of dreams. His work underpins most of what we know today on the subject. While Jung acknowledged his debt to Freud, he disagreed with him on two important points: first, whether the dream was always and necessarily the imaging of a wish fulfilment, and second, in the light of that, how a dream should be anatomised for interpretation.

Jung felt that dreams were, more simply, 'a spontaneous self-portrayal, in symbolic form, of the actual situation in the unconscious' (1985, p. 49). He rejected Freud's theoretical split between latent and manifest content, and believed instead that the dream was its own context.

Consequently, he did not use free association to arrive at meaning; rather, he insisted that each dream be examined carefully in the light of the symbols it presented and the meaning that the dreamer gave to those symbols. 'The whole dream work is essentially subjective, and a dream is a theatre in which the dreamer is himself the scene, the player, the prompter, the producer, the author, the public, and the critic' (1985, p. 52).

For both Freud and Jung, interpreting a dream was like interpreting a difficult piece of text, which inevitably needed the input of the author — the dreamer — to attain any real enlightenment.

Apart from introducing dreams to a wider audience and extending Freud's work in the area, Jung's greatest achievement was to connect the work of psychoanalysis, including the analysis of dreams, with broader studies of mythology, anthropology, religion and art. He conceived the idea of archetypes (see chapter three) and he made exhaustive studies of ancient texts, mythologies and symbols. Jung linked primitive man's intuition about dreams with the findings of modern science. Both, for him, were right: '... [C]ontemporary man ... is blind to the fact that, with all his rationality and efficiency, he is possessed by

"powers" that are beyond his control. His gods and demons have not disappeared at all; they have merely got new names. They keep him on the run with restlessness, vague apprehensions, psychological complications ...'(1978, p. 71).

On the other hand, and perhaps not surprisingly for one of such impressive and yet communicable erudition, Jung maintained a robust respect for man's conscious abilities: 'If the unconscious really were superior to consciousness it would be difficult to see wherein the advantage of consciousness lay ...' (1978, p. 82). However, he pointed out that man's conscious component has only evolved relatively recently, and is far from complete. Unconsciousness, he said, is 'the undeniable inheritance of all mankind ... What we call the "psyche" is by no means identical with consciousness and its contents' (1978, p. 6).

Today, much headway is being made in the study of dreams as we explore the nature of the psyche. With the increasing complexities and demands of modern life, it is perhaps even more essential that we accept the messages that our dreams convey. It is important for all dreaming souls to watch and interpret the signals from their unconscious, which links us with ourselves, each other, and the cosmos.

2
The characteristics of dreams

AMBIGUITY AND LACK OF NARRATIVE

To our waking minds, dreams are ambiguous and confusing. They present us with bizarre arrangements of characters and situations, and often lack any logical sense of narrative. Time, place and even the laws of gravity are defied. Animals speak to us; objects move, otherwise familiar and likeable characters behave monstrously; strangers pursue or help us; we visit unknown but fully realised landscapes.

It is for this reason that dreams are so often forgotten on waking. The waking mind finds its night-time journeyings difficult to follow and in the cold, logical

Those who have compared our life to a dream were, by chance, more right than they thought… We are awake while we are sleeping, and sleeping while awake.

– Michel de Montaigne

light of day, dreams seem like blurred phantasms. Like a thin pall of mist, they form a veil between our conscious life and that other part of our psyche to which we have less access and of which we may be a bit afraid. Like mist, dreams evaporate under the heat of sunrise and the intellect, leaving only a sense that we have travelled in terrain that is deeply familiar and yet profoundly opaque, accessible only through the portals of sleep.

Unless we learn to remember. And the only way to do this is to accept the special illogic of dreams, and work with it. That is, to expand our sense of this other world that exists within every single one of us; a world that reflects, albeit through cryptic metaphor and mystifying associations, the very foundations of our Self. That is, to chart the dream terrain, and begin to understand the significance of the signposts we create for ourselves every night.

Through memory comes access. But our conscious memory is so used to compartmentalising and fixing facts in linear structures and acceptable language that the fantastical leaps, twists and jargon of dreams seem impossibly illusory, even when our daytime recall is relatively strong. Generally speaking, we hold onto what we comprehend and what is useful, and sometimes dreams seem just plain silly, or embarrassing, or that special dream combination of highly unpleasant and highly improbable. It is then easy to dismiss our dreams as meaningless mind-buzz after a busy day. What is dismissed rarely will be recalled.

Acceptance of the contrarieties and incongruities of dreams is the first step to comprehension. Dreams do not arise from the logical continuity of daily experience, but are indicative of a totally different sort of psychic activity which takes place only in sleep. The fantastical nature of the associations made in dreams, and their tenuous connection with what we normally term 'reality', makes their narrative, such as it exists at all, extremely unstable. When recording dreams, it is important to bear this in mind. Try not to impose order where none exists. As you become more sensitive to your dreams and more adept at interpreting them for yourself, you will discover the keys to your dreams. These keys lie in the nature of the symbols and motifs presented to you and even more importantly, the feelings you have associated with them. These elements, which are tied in a more or less significant way to your daily activities, provide the cornerstones of meaning in dream interpretation.

Acceptance of the peculiar language of dreams — pictographic, metaphorical, allusive — will give you the key. It is simply not sufficient to look for objectives, probabilities or familiar behaviours. Nor is it sufficient to make facile equations. If in your dream your mother is cavorting aboard a purple elephant who is trumpeting sophisticated sonnets at you, or someone like you, it does not necessarily mean that Mum is about to take a dangerous trip to India!

And yet, as angels in

some brighter dreams

Call to the soul

when man doth

sleep,

So some strange

thought transcend

our wonted themes,

And into glory peep.

– HENRY VAUGHAN, *'ASCENSION-HYMN'*

CREATIVITY

We have all been touched by works of art in any genre – painting, music, poetry, films, for example – that somehow bridge the gap between the conscious and the unconscious, that draw back the veil. They show us a concrete waking example of the power of the dream image through the potent language of symbols — the concept discussed in depth in chapter one. How is it that artists can access and reproduce dream images with such clarity and immediacy?

Artists accept and explore the recesses of their night minds and pay a great deal of attention to their dreams — examining them, drawing from them, and honing their ability to re-vision and refashion them in waking life. Works that are bizarre, disturbing, illogical or even puzzling nevertheless exhibit the peculiar power and depth of the dream-inspired imagination.

Two examples will illustrate this. The symbolists of the late nineteenth century venerated the relationship between their creative imaginations and their art. The 'dream' for them was both a personal and a cultural vision, implying a freedom from established principles. It denoted a subjective and inventive view of the world which they were free to express in any form or style they wished. Actual dreams were frequently represented in painting, sculpture, poetry and music.

Half a century later, the surrealists took their impetus from the development of psychoanalysis to allow them free rein in expressing the visions and desires of the unconscious, seen in often bizarre juxtapositions. Once again, like the symbolists, they exalted the powerful inspiration of imagination and dream.

To this day, the lasting legacy of these two movements survives. The arts in all forms accept and explore the interior landscape of the artist, and the nature of imagination.

Most of us are familiar with Albert Einstein's famous dictum, 'Imagination is more important than knowledge'. Many scientists working on the edge of discoveries about the natural world have been given crucial clues about their research in dreams. Einstein stated that a dream he had as a young man inspired his scientific research for the rest of his illustrious career. In the dream, he was sleighing down a mountainside at the speed of light. He noticed that the stars refracted light into a spectrum of colours. Einstein maintained that thinking deeply about this dream brought him to the theory of relativity.

Other scientists have recorded extraordinary insights brought to them in their dreams, after they have struggled for years with complex new theories. The dreams bring the flash needed to complete the picture and solve the problem.

We would do well to learn from societies whose harmony with nature and themselves is an attribute largely lost to twentieth-century Westerners. There are still tribal societies that respect and listen to their dreams, giving them a central role in their culture. The Naskapi Indians of the Labrador Peninsula in Canada rely on dreams in their everyday life. Jung related that these tribes believe in an inner being called Mista-Peo, who directs the individual life in its solitary existence. The Naskapi often live alone, and listening to the promptings of Mista-Peo is regarded as essential for a whole life. They believe that the more one takes note of his teachings, the better and more helpful one's dreams become.

In Australia, the Aboriginal tribes accord huge importance to the process of dreaming. Their mythological system translates in English as 'the Dreaming'. Robert Lawlor, in his book *Voices of the First Day,* discusses the concept at length. He points out that Aboriginal initiation includes teachings on how to move between conscious and unconscious worlds through trance states. 'Sleep is but one entrance into The Dreaming. Becoming increasingly lucid in sleep ... is the beginning of the initiation process for every tribal person' (1991, p. 50).

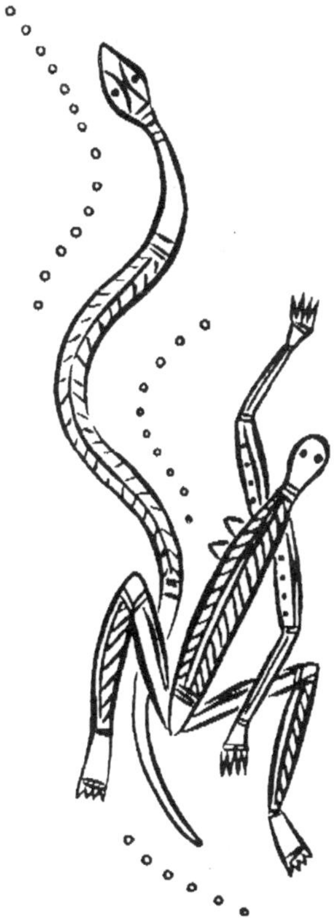

The intellect has assumed an overweening importance in the lives of civilised people. It dries up the fertile mists of our dreams and, in doing so, dries out the imagination. Imagination and creativity feed on unconscious processes. And while the operation of the intellect is one of our most admirable attributes, and essential for the ordering and onward trajectory of our minds and daily lives, the death of the imagination in our culture is a sad thing to behold. It signals the death of personal creativity, intuition and a deeply felt joy in the sense of Self.

The Aborigines maintain that white people have 'lost their Dreaming'. For them, the Dreaming is an organic vision of the world that extends beyond concrete reality. 'No objective can be of greater significance for human survival than the recovery of the Dreaming. The Aboriginal way of life and the Aboriginal revelation hold the seeds for the rebirth of the Dreamtime in humanity' (Lawlor 1991, p. 385).

DISGUISE

Apart from the general feelings and incongruities associated with the dream state, there are other characteristics of dreams that must be noted before you set off on a journey of interpretation.

Remember that the dream can assume the nature of a disguise. This is due to three factors.

The first factor is our natural tendency to repress complexes or any unpleasant material (see chapter one, and more on this later). A dream may shock us deeply

Was it a vision, or

a waking dream?

Fled is that music:–

Do I wake or sleep?

– JOHN KEATS, *ODE TO A NIGHTINGALE*

because it blithely shows us images that are completely at odds with our conscious thoughts.

My dream began with me lying in bed looking at the floor when a rather beautiful golden snake emerged from under my previous day's clothes. While I was watching this incredible snake coming towards me, a common, everyday tarantula emerged from the other side of the clothing (I am terrified of these spiders). Then my dream changed and my husband and I were being handed some beautifully coloured birds. These birds were a cross between a rooster and a giant pigeon. Not one of the birds had the same coloured feathers; they were all mixed and there was brilliant plumage everywhere. Someone told me to hold the birds upside down, which I did. Then they started exploding, one by one. I was covered with brightly coloured goo from the exploded birds and I woke up in a panic.

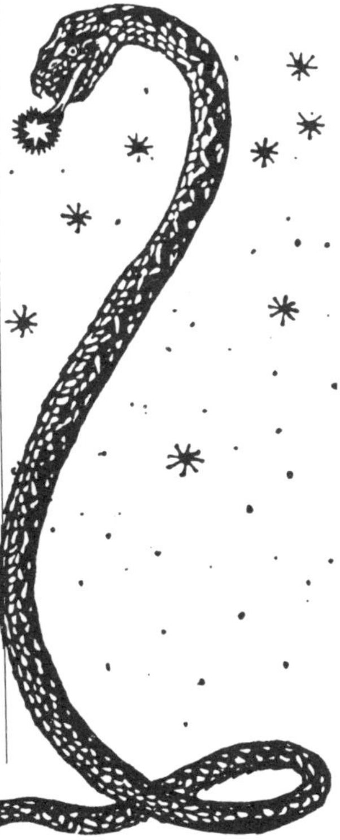

The golden snake depicts supreme spiritual determination. Seeing the snake uncoiling from your clothes suggests a spiritual and sexual awakening. The snake is related to birds in the evolutionary ladder. The suggestion here may be that you will be able to soar to higher regions once you fulfil your inner feelings either spiritually or sexually. In pre-Columbian America there was a much-revered image of the 'plumed serpent': a snake with feathers on its

I had a dream the other night that my husband was following me through a dense forest to a small swimming pool. He reached into the pool and a baby hippopotamus swallowed him up.

The hippo represents strength and vigour, and in myth is related to the horse. The forest didn't swallow you up, but it depicts complexity. Having survived the forest your husband was lost to emotion and overpowered by the hippo. Is it you that is always the one to take the lead in the marriage? Let your husband fend for you occasionally.

head and tail and sometimes on its body. The brilliance of the colours contained in your dream relates to high energy levels and is symbolic of your natural self. The spider may be the other side of the equation. It emerges from the other side of the clothing. We all have a dark side, one that we fear and largely choose to ignore. In myth, the spider is related to the moon.

The second factor is that the dream is not a thought. It is an image floating up from a subliminal state, complete in itself. As such, it is not subject to the strictures of the conscious. It is pre-conscious and has no truck with time, place or demeanour. The images the dream presents have their own sufficiency and are specific to the message it is conveying. In this way, the images are like a parable or metaphor to the dreamer.

The third factor is that a dream is full of images that are condensed. This term was first used and expanded by Freud. The meaning I give it is that certain intensely charged thoughts will often compress themselves into one symbol, which, by virtue of its intense and collective nature, may often be difficult to decipher at first glance.

I recently had a very disturbing dream in which the sun plummeted to earth, causing an eclipse and total darkness. There were fires, burnt people panicking to escape the fires, death and total mayhem. I am still amazed that I had such a morbid and depressing dream. When I am pregnant I have dreams that are much more vivid and wild than usual.

Your dream really is a good dream. The sun represents the positive and also signifies essential warmth and nourishment for people and the earth. Witnessing the sun plummeting in such a way could signify purification and the destruction of evil forces. It could also mean that your sense of passion is overwhelming, and can be destructive as well as nurturing. Dreams during pregnancy can be more vivid than usual due to hormonal changes. REM sleep is reported to be longer than usual and this results in a banquet of dreams that are more complex and often much sexier than usual.

I dreamt that I looked in the mirror to examine my teeth and they seemed to be growing bigger and overcrowding my mouth. I was trying to push them back in as I was no longer able to keep them in place. There was blood on my gums and my mouth wouldn't shut properly, but no teeth actually fell out.

Looking in the mirror and seeing your overcrowded mouth full of teeth suggests that you could be facing an identity crisis. Teeth in dreams often point to a fear of ageing, a loss of image, but as there was blood it could be that what you were concerned about is finished. This dream does reflect an anxiety associated with either the original loss of baby teeth or a neglect on the part of the dreamer to care for their teeth. An inadequate diet and use of bad speech or language is also connected with a dream of teeth.

MORALITY

A dream does not conform to any morality, although it may say a great deal about the feelings about morality held by the dreamer. For example, you, the dreamer, could be happily making love with someone completely unknown or inappropriate, without sex having anything at all to do with what the dream actually signifies. On the other hand, an obscure dream may hold some significance for your erotic life but be not at all erotic in image. This very well could be because the eroticism in question is an uncomfortable issue for the dreamer to deal with, and so the dream employs its usual technique of metaphor.

COMPENSATION

If we take note of Jung's statement that dreams are a mirror of the actual state of the unconscious, then we can accept that the whole direction of dreams is to compensate for imbalances that exist. This is sometimes rather unpleasant for the dreamer. As mentioned earlier, dreams often point to complexes and unresolved vulnerabilities that will have been carefully and ruthlessly covered up by the dreamer. Often it does not seem to be in the best interests of the conscious to bring these difficulties to light. So, unfortunately, the allusive and metaphoric language of dreams works against itself. It is hard for the unconscious to bludgeon the conscious soul into recognition of imbalances, except through the desperate agency of terrible nightmares, recurring dreams or, in extreme cases, insertions into the conscious life in the form of neuroses and obsessions. In all these cases one can be sure that something serious is afoot and simply must be examined for the dreamer to obtain relief.

It is difficult to make any more generalised statements on the compensatory nature of dreams because each person will have not only their own unique constellation of images with which their dreams work, but also a unique and complex personality that may need different things at different times in their lives. Once again, we are up against the fact that self-examination by the dreamer is important, because it is from the minutiae of a person's own existence and challenges that their dream images will arise.

PROJECTION

Projection, a term used frequently in psychoanalysis, has considerable bearing on our dream lives. It is important for you, the dreamer, to grasp the concept, without having to enter the debate that has taken place on the subject.

Projection is essential and normal. It happens all the time. It is, in short, the tendency to identify certain powerful feelings with an object (often with another person, a place, or a thing). Primitive people unconsciously projected mythic meaning into their environment. Usually, unfavourable projections are outside our most intimate circle: they are unfavourable and unpleasant, therefore they are not close. Favourable projections are saved for our close friends, lovers, and relatives, although most of us confuse the good with the bad at some stage. If I am uncomfortable with feelings of rage, then I will find someone or something on which to project it. I may choose someone distant (a politician, an ex-partner, a boss) who is in a rage all the time, which defuses my own rage and makes me feel quite smug. Of course, there are usually significant traces of the projected feeling in the object of projection. The politician, ex-partner or boss will probably be full of rage. If this were not the case — if we chose to project rage into a shy neighbour or the Pope — then we would simply be fanciful, if not nuts.

Taking rage as the example again, I may choose to connect with someone whose behaviour is outrageous, so that my anger is justified. They misbehave, I become enraged. Then they become enraged, they misbehave, I become enraged. This latter projection is becoming dangerously neurotic: I am enraged, but equally *need* to be enraged to discharge an old psychic wound. I am bound to the projection, and this is damaging. It is for this reason that neurotics seek help, because their projections in even their immediate circle lead to bitter conflict.

However, in most people, the good projections are close, the bad ones further away. Jung calls them, aptly, 'a bridge of

illusion across which love and hate can stream off so relievingly' (1985, p. 58). They are illusions, but they are not problematic. They are even necessary: how many people could begin and end every emotion only with themselves?

Projections are significant in terms of the interpretation of the dreams, as all emotions in dreams are personified or objectified.They are symbolised. We may see our body as a house, or a car; the state of our emotions as the sea; our fear as a monster or a frightening animal. Certain people may appear in our dreams imbued with unfamiliar feelings. Our minds may create unknown people or give dearly known and loved people horrible attributes. The dream may invent a benign spider, even though the dreamer is normally terrified of them.

But projections work in a sort of inverse way in dreams: they may elucidate certain things that we do not see, or they may help us to see our true, subjective feelings about someone or some situation which previously seemed unclear or even unimportant. It is crucial when interpreting dreams to pay great attention to the subjective. That is why you, the dreamer, need to take an active role in interpretation.

Personification is a very important method employed by the unconscious in dreams. It is a way for the unconscious to examine the relative values of the personality of the dreamer, which are expressed figuratively in the dream: that is, certain aspects of the personality take on a life of their own. Thus, for example, the feminine aspect of a male dreamer may be indicated by the presence of a woman in the dream, and vice versa for a female dreamer. These figures are not separate from the dreamer; rather, they are elements of the self that are being represented. The imaging, role-playing aspect of the unconscious creates these projections in our dreams to dramatise our personal concerns and dilemmas. While these figures are not necessarily recognisable to the dreamer, they carry with them a deep sense of familiarity.

The projective nature of the dream becomes extremely powerful when we

enter the realm of archetypes, which express both aspects of the self and aspects of the universal unconscious. This is explained further in chapter three.

CONNECTION WITH DAILY EVENTS

One other very important fact about dreams is that although they may employ memory fragments from forgotten episodes, they are almost always connected with the experiences of the preceding day. So there will be some link that connects seemingly irrelevant material with very recent history. That history may not be an actual event in time: it may instead be a train of preoccupying thought or impression. And while the event or thought may be represented through some negligible memory fragment, in the words of Freud, 'nothing that has really remained indifferent can be reproduced in a dream' (1958, p. 269).

For this reason, when keeping a dream diary, it is very important to note down the events and major preoccupations and thoughts of the preceding day. (Chapter seven provides a detailed regime of how to remember and interpret your dreams.)

We are such stuff

As dreams are made

on, and our little life

Is rounded with a

sleep!

– WILLIAM SHAKESPEARE, *THE TEMPEST*

3
Archetypes, symbols and dreams

WHAT IS AN ARCHETYPE?

The set of symbols known as *archetypes* needs to be evaluated in any comprehensive discussion on dreams and their interpretation. Archetype is a term first used by Jung.

An archetype is a symbolic motif that expresses itself in the same essential pattern across all cultures, religions and classes. The form of each archetype will be specific to each individual, tribe or social group. Archetypes are inherited, primordial images that appear spontaneously from the depths of our unconscious. Archetypal motifs appear frequently in art, and they are often expressed in individual dreams. Their peculiar power resides in the fact

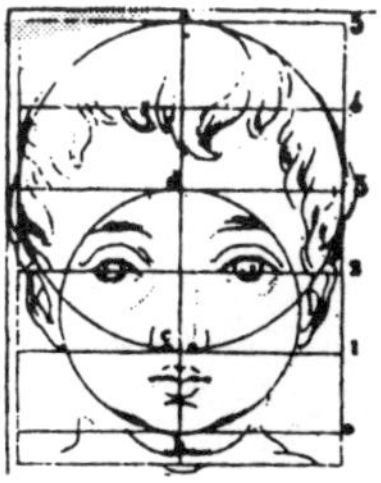

Consciousness reigns but does not govern.

–Paul Valery

that they are unconscious manifestations of primitive instincts and aspirations. They can take many forms, and are often personalised in the artist's or dreamer's vision. Essentially, however, they are a primitive constellation of symbols that are intimately connected to the precognitive area of the psyche (the greater part of the psyche).

Archetypes are by nature collective. They appear everywhere in human discourse, ancient and modern, whether that discourse is art, literature, tribal ritual or the dreams of an urban and thoroughly civilised individual of the late twentieth century. Archetypes are thus related closely to myth, which is the storytelling component of our collective history. We could characterise myths as the external ordering of the *collective unconscious* (Jung's term again). And the collective unconscious is the domain of the archetype.

ARCHETYPAL DREAMS

While the existence of archetypal dreams has been generally accepted by the community of researchers on dreams, their significance and application has always been under some dispute. In short, many theorists on dreams are wary of using archetypal symbols in the interpretation of specific dreams, feeling that the parameters of these types of symbols are difficult to quantify in context. Many find the metaphysical abstraction inherent in any description of archetypes too unwieldy and too inclined to lead away from the real implications of the particular dream in question, rather than illuminating and aiding interpretation. While I believe that archetypes must be applied with care in any interpretation of a dream, I have not been as mistrustful of them as some of my colleagues.

Archetypal dreams have much in common with the concerns of ancient myths: the cycles of death and rebirth, the ascendance of the Hero, initiation rites, the creation of the world, and the journey (particularly the sea voyage).

Paradoxically, or perhaps even ironically, archetypes can only be described conceptually. The forms of the Anima/Animus (see page 57), the Wise Elder, the Great Mother or the Mandala, for example, will be specific to each individual, or at least each tribe or social group. This makes sense, as the archetype needs to be personified to have meaning. In other words, the universal symbol carried fluidly and formlessly in the collective unconscious precipitates out into the art or ritual created by a tribe or society to describe their identity, or into the dreams created by the individual psyche. Archetypal images clearly demonstrate universal patterns but, like all dream symbols, are significant to the individual only when they fuse with his or her particular emotional make-up. Once again, like symbols, archetypes need to be examined in the light of the entire life situation of the dreamer.

In dream therapy, we find that troubling images usually disappear from the individual's dream repertoire once the issues they depict are examined and fully understood by the dreamer. This is not the case with archetypes. Archetypes always have universal significance. The contents of the archetype can be assimilated by the individual, but the generic image always remains, floating around the collective unconscious.

Archetypes are powerful but shadowy (the Shadow figure is one of the most significant of them). The dreamer will remember quite vividly a nocturnal brush with an archetype — such is their importance — even if unable to fathom the exact significance. Jung called dreams in which archetypes play a major role 'big dreams'. These dreams are experienced at times of change or crisis, or to mark the progressive stages of puberty, initiation and maturity, or to herald the spiritual landmarks of life.

This all seems a bit hard to swallow at first; a clever and complex system, but somehow implausible. The thought that each of us is plugged into a collective unconscious will be alarming for some readers. Most of us only connect consciously with the so-called Primitive Mind in a sort of nostalgia for Paradise Lost. However, the dangers of what could be called our Sophisticated Dislocation have been discussed. The archetype is one of the most powerful legacies of our unconscious heritage.

ARCHETYPAL DREAMS AND THE HUMAN PSYCHE

If we contemplate the sheer volume of time involved in the evolution of the human psyche, the phenomenon of the inherited archetype becomes easier to comprehend.

For the first 60,000 years of history, humans were dependent on their instincts for survival. They developed innate thought patterns that corresponded with their instincts, and promoted successful evolution.

It is only in the past 8000 years or so that humans have become 'civilised'; that is to say, people's minds have been concerned with more than subsistence and avoiding predators larger than themselves.

Jung summed up the developments of the psyche succinctly. He said that 'We should laugh at the idea of a plant or an animal inventing itself, yet there are many people who believe that the psyche or mind invented itself and thus was the creator of its own existence ... the mind has grown to its present state of consciousness as an acorn grows into an oak or as saurians developed into mammals. As it has for so long been developing, so it still develops, and thus we are moved by forces from within as well as by stimuli from without' (1978, p. 71).

Joseph Campbell, the great mythologist, described archetypes as 'an order of psychological laws inhering in the structure of the body, which has not radically altered since the period of the Aurignacian caves and can be as readily identified in the jungles of Brazil as in the cafes of Paris, as readily in the igloos of Baffin Land as in the harems of Marrakech' (1959,p. 33). Just as the human anatomy shows unmistakable vestiges of our heritage, so does the mind. We know that the human infant, like other infant animals, is preprogrammed in certain ways. The adult human mind, also, is preprogrammed in certain ways. Our instincts are still with us, and manifest themselves, psychically, in archetypal symbols that are powerful motivators, imprints or signals which have their roots in our collective past.

If any reader still doubts the existence and importance of archetypal dreams, one last fact should be sufficient: young children can have vivid archetypal dreams. The key symbols of these dreams refer clearly to elements of which the child cannot possibly have had knowledge. These are not tales told in the playground, or even taken from fairytales.

CHARACTERISTICS OF ARCHETYPAL DREAMS

An archetypal dream is usually the representation of a seminal change or shift in the psyche of the dreamer. It is often recalled with great clarity. Another characteristic of archetypal dreams is that the dreamer usually feels that he or she has received a 'higher' wisdom, in whatever form, from an outside source. The archetypal symbol may not correspond with any usual dream connectors — like familiar events, personalities, situations or memories — but carries with it a sense of great significance. There is something about archetypal dreams — whether frightening, confusing or peaceful — which inspires a sense of awe in the dreamer.

Archetypes take many forms. They are often personifications: the *Anima* (female figure) or *Animus* (male figure); the *Shadow* (usually a figure that carries sinister connotations), the *Trickster,* the *Wise Old Man or Wise Old Woman,* or the *Divine Child.* They can also be abstract motifs like *mandalas* (magic circles), which will occur in dreams in forms such as flowers, configurations in a landscape, or even objects. Certain animals, most notably the snake, seem to be archetypal (see page 87). The journey is a common archetypal theme that marks the passage of the individual's development.

COMMON ARCHETYPES

Four archetypes appear most frequently in dreams and hold a particular significance for all dreamers. These are the Shadow, the Persona, the Anima/Animus and Dream Babies.

Other key archetypal images are covered in chapter four.

THE SHADOW

Usually seen as a definite dream personality with a sinister aspect, the Shadow expresses all that we would like to forget or deny about ourselves. It usually manifests as a figure of the same sex as the dreamer. Jung thought that the Shadow also embodies all the more undeveloped aspects of the human psyche, the urges that are negative in character; greed, lust, hate and violence are good examples. The force of these hidden or repressed urges in the unconscious can make the Shadow a very potent figure indeed when it appears in our dreams.

Like all archetypes, the Shadow works on two levels: the universal and the personal. Inevitably, both sides are shown in the individual dreamer's manifestation. So even if the personal aspects of the Shadow are acknowledged, discussed and integrated, it will never disappear entirely. This is because it represents something larger than the individual – the history of the human person's negative or problematic desires stands behind it. This gives the Shadow a particularly active charge, and is probably the reason why it usually appears first among all the archetypes in any individual's dream analysis over a period of time.

The awful shadow of some unseen Power Floats though unseen among us.

– PERCY BYSSHE SHELLEY, *'HYMN TO INTELLECTUAL BEAUTY'*

Throughout my childhood I have dreamt that I am sleeping in my bed and a tall man dressed in black is watching over me. I cannot see his face. I still have the same dream occasionally. I wake up feeling scared because the dream seems so real.

This type of dreaming is connected with the darker side of self. It is the Shadow of self who is standing by your bed. Many dream this way and frighten themselves, but there is no need to feel fear. It is simply that the tall dark man depicts the side you keep hidden from others.

The Shadow appears frequently in bad dreams or nightmares (see page 134). It can appear as a pursuer, a bringer of bad news, or any other threatening figure. In whatever form, the Shadow is usually tied up with a feeling of fear.

Accepting our own dark side can be extremely difficult. This is another reason why the Shadow is so potent. It comes back to remind us again and again that all the unpleasantness and downright horror of which humankind is capable is buried inside the unconscious of each one of us. The Shadow is a savage.

'Unfortunately, there can be no doubt that man is, on the whole, less good than he imagines himself or wants to be,' remarked Jung (Storr 1983, p. 88). 'Everyone carries a Shadow, and the less it is embodied in the individual's conscious life, the blacker and denser it is.' Thus overtly pious or energetically 'good' people are often found to have a brutal 'dark' side that overcomes them from time to time because it is not integrated into their conscious personality.

For most of us, the Shadow appears in daily life as tantrums, being beastly to one's mate, behaving selfishly, telling lies, drinking to excess, gossiping nastily, or even eating three blocks of chocolate instead of one. So our Shadow side is not neccessarily *evil,* although repression can make it so. As Jung points out, 'it even contains childish or primitive qualities which would in a way vitalise or embellish human existence, but convention forbids!' (Storr 1983, p. 90).

As the dark is the inverse of the light, the Shadow is intimately connected to our moral sense. It certainly takes strong moral effort to examine oneself and recognise the dark aspects of our Shadow as real aspects of our selves – real in conscious life. Dreams are easily distanced in the light of day.

Our primary distancing technique is, of course, projection. The Shadow is often projected onto others around us, and may appear in our dreams with the face of someone we dislike. The characteristics we most ardently detest or loudly condemn in others often exist, unacknowledged, within us. It is much more comfortable to see them out there, operating in the detestable or lamentable personality of someone else. People who are used as scapegoats are often subject to this sort of projection.

This is not a conscious decision, but rather the way in which the unconscious deals with its most unsavoury aspects. The more the Shadow is integrated into conscious life, the less the projection will be. The more the Shadow is integrated, the less it pursues us in our dreams.

In my dream I saw a hooded figure just standing with a very dark background. I couldn't see the face of the figure. The figure moved as if to grab me; I felt it grab me and I screamed. As I woke, my husband was standing at the foot of the bed and he said I looked so scared.

The Shadow beside your bed represents your other self trying to get in touch with you. We must all recognise that we have two sides of self; your black figure is faceless because you have not yet recognised this fact. Your dream produced fear, so try to work out what or who may be stopping you from showing what you really feel about a person or place.

THE PERSONA

Essentially, the Persona is our mask. While society deems it necessary for us to present a cohesive face to the world, it is often at the risk of losing touch with other, equally important, elements of ourselves. 'A man cannot get rid of himself in favour of an artificial persona without punishment,' said Jung (Storr 1983, p. 95). When there is too much identification with the mask, then usually there are compensations in the private life, and often families suffer the real state of affairs. Thus, for example, we may see the pillar-of-society husband (who pursues clandestine nocturnal interests on the side) with a sick, reclusive or mentally unstable wife; or a 'perfect' family with one drug-addicted child.

The Persona is not subjective – that is, it is not produced from our impressions or intuitions or inner state. Rather, it is a useful objective tool developed by the Ego to relate to the requirements of the world, society and our ambitions. This in itself is not a problem: the Persona only becomes problematic when it replaces the Self in

So may the outward shows be least themselves:

The world is still deceived with ornament.

– WILLIAM SHAKESPEARE, *THE MERCHANT OF VENICE*

all its complexity. Then, the Persona can become a tyrannical, rigid construct.

An overactive Persona may give rise to dreams in which the dreamer appears naked, or is ostracised in some way.

I have had this dream a few times and it really shocks me. I have a very good job as a private secretary and in my dream I am at work, dressed exactly as I would be usually but without my blouse. I am working away doing my regular jobs and nobody takes any notice of me. I am decked out with just a bra and a skirt. This dream leaves me feeling very confused and embarrassed as I am very conservative!

Your dream is the opposite of how you see yourself and depicts you being exposed. Many dreamers see themselves partly clothed or naked. It represents a fear of being seen for what they really are. At work

you may cultivate the image of Miss Perfect. Do you have a secret wish to be seen as something else? Your dream is dramatising this sort of hidden dilemma.

THE ANIMA/ANIMUS

Just as the Persona looks outward to the world, the Anima (for men) or Animus (for women) represents the inner face of the psyche. In essence, the Anima/Animus has qualities that are complementary to the gender of the Persona. Thus, for a man, the Anima is the inner feminine, and for a woman, the Animus is the inner masculine. Both of these inner complements form part of the whole Self.

In dreams, they are personified in images of a woman or a man. The sex will be the opposite to that of the dreamer.

Generally speaking, the relationship the dreamer has with the parent of the opposite sex will set the tone of the Anima/Animus. The role that the dreamer ascribes to their gender will also play a large part in determining the nature of the archetype. So, a man who shows an aggressively masculine Persona will have a soft and feminine Anima dream image. This is because the more that masculine traits are

All dreams of the soul

End in a beautiful man's or woman's body.

– W.B. YEATS

expressed in the outer attitude, the more any feminine traits must be repressed. The feminine is consigned to the unconscious, from whence it wells up in dreams. The same process in opposition holds true for a woman and her Animus (see Erotic dreams on page 109).

We see everywhere references to the romantic ideal — the man or woman of our dreams. This is basically how the Anima/ Animus figures are expressed in the world around us. They are strong archetypal ideals. The problem is that most of us at some stage or another project these ideals out, onto another person. Thus, just as we project our Shadow onto other people, we project our Anima/Animus onto the man or woman of our dreams.

This is romantic love. According to Jung, 'whenever an impassioned, almost magical relationship exists between the sexes, it is invariably a question of a projected soul-image' (Storr 1983, p. 104). This is all very well, if it accommodates a real and lasting relationship, but problematic if it leads to dependency and despair.

In the individual, the Anima/Animus expresses the person's other side. A man's Anima is expressed in sentiment and emotion, intuition and other 'feminine' qualities. Just how these qualities are expressed, and to what degree, depends on whether he is in touch enough with his internal feminine. If a man is comfortable with his internal feminine, then he will have no difficulty in consciously expressing these qualities. If, on the other hand, these qualities are repressed, then his Anima may

trouble him in his dreams, and he may form misalliances with women who correspond with the feminine he rejects in himself.

For women, the Animus expresses determination, ambition, logic, opinion — all strong, 'masculine' qualities. The effect of her repression or integration of these characteristics in herself will be the same as for a man and his Anima.

For people who have started to wrestle with their internal genders and who have experienced the wonder and confusion of romantic love, the Anima/Animus of their dreams can be a wonderful guide, showing them where to focus their energies to make themselves whole and content, and allowing them to have the fulfilling and stable relationships that lie beyond the thrill of falling in love.

I am madly in love with a woman. I am a woman and I love and dream about my wonderful woman lover. We used to be so much in love. We have been separated for over a year now. I am always dreaming about her and myself. When I dream about her we are always getting back together. The dreams are very real and colourful. I want so much for my dreams to come true as I finally found someone of my own kind to love. I am trying hard to get along without her but hoping and praying that my dreams may come true. Are my dreams confirming that we are soulmates, as I do believe in that sort of thing? Please help me, as these dreams are really hurting.

Ordinarily, if you dream of making love to someone of the same sex, it indicates finding the confidence to begin your own thing! You have declared your sexuality and therefore loving some one of the same sex relates to you experiencing a desire to return to your feelings that have been cut off. As soulmates it is possible for you always to remain friends. However, this may not be good enough for you or your friend. Move on and make a physical effort to meet new people and attract a new lover.

For many years now I (a man) have had a recurring dream that I am dressed in ladies' attire, with all the garments that a woman wears, from foundation to high-heeled shoes. I wear a straight skirt, about calf length. Over this, I wear one or two ladies' bib aprons which enwrap the entire get-up. I seem to feel great and comfortable and I always have a lot of people around me in various situations. No-one seems to notice my unusual gear except myself. When I wake up I am appalled, for I have no desire to realise my dream, not even in the privacy of my own home. I hope you have an explanation for this type of situation for me.

You should look at this dream with humour and not with disapproval. As it is recurring it would be interesting to note what happens on the day of the dream. It is almost like a dream of being naked. You may be an extrovert in real life, and dress well, as a man, yet your dream shows you in opposite mode. Probably, the dream is just showing you feeling comfortably at home with your feminine side, in which case it is a very positive dream. The presence of other people who do not notice your unusual garb supports this. Or it may be that the dream is encouraging you to show hidden desires and fantasies that you might otherwise be uncomfortable demonstrating.

DREAM BABIES

Dreams of having a baby or being pregnant may be common to women of child-bearing age, but this type of dream does not necessarily mean that a pregnancy is in the offing. Men may also dream of babies, and some even dream of being pregnant.

Dream babies prefigure the genesis of a new creative spirit in your life. This may take the form of a special new project, or even the appearance of an important new person. Of course, if you are focused on having a family, then the important new person may well be a newborn.

Some months before two important new events occurred in my life, I had a vivid dream about two babies for whom I was caring. They seemed to me to be twins. One baby was chattering happily, while the other watched me, smiling. I was wrapping them up warmly in bunny rugs. I awoke with the feeling that significant events were imminent. Shortly afterwards, I signed a contract to write this book, just before I left on a study trip to the United States and England. While I was in New York, days

When the first baby laughed for the first time, the laugh broke into a thousand pieces and they all went skipping about, and that was the beginning of fairies.

– J.M. BARRIE, *PETER PAN*

before I was due to leave for London, I learnt that I had been granted an interview (for a forthcoming project) with Diana, the Princess of Wales. I had felt sure that my babies were positive messengers from my unconscious, and my instincts had been confirmed. These were two pet projects that I had been nurturing (wrapping them up in bunny rugs) for some time.

It is interesting that, even with the dramatic changes in women's roles over the past 60 years, dream babies still harbour such potent and primal symbolism. A woman's body remains a woman's body, and the eternal rhythms of her menstrual cycle and gestation phases generate key symbolic links between conscious and unconscious. For example, women often dream of babies at the time of ovulation, indicating that their bodies are 'ripe' and receptive. These dreams should be reassuring at a very deep level, even if the woman has no desire at that particular time to fall pregnant. However, take heed. Dreams are potent. It may be worth reviewing your feelings on your own fertility, or taking extra care with contraception! When a woman is intent on starting or continuing a family, then wish-fulfilment babies may people her dreams. With a family of four grown

For the second time in twelve months I dreamt that I was about 6 months pregnant and both times I felt pleased with myself and very, very special. I remember when I awoke that I felt good about myself and very contented.

Non-pregnant women dreaming this way may be experiencing the birth of a new idea. This could be a very good time for you right now with your work. An important project could be likened to your child! Many creative people will talk about their projects in terms of gestation periods, birth and growth. Your dream is positive, because it leaves you with a feeling of contentment.

children behind me, I knew that my dream babies were not of this genre. They were indicative of other creative endeavours that were coming to fruition.

Men's baby dreams often fall into the latter category. However, because pregnancy and babies are so strongly associated with the female domain, when a male has such dreams it usually holds special significance in terms of his relationship with his own 'eternal feminine', or anima, and the creativity embraced therein (see page 57).

If a man dreams he is pregnant, it may be that he is undergoing some crucial unconscious questioning about his relationship to his anima. This does not necessarily mean he is questioning his gender preferences, rather that he is busy relating his masculinity to his own internal feminine blueprint. Pregnancy is a powerful feminine symbol of fecundity. In contrast, typical male dreams of potency, particularly in youth, tend to focus on identifiably phallic motifs. So a pregnancy dream may be both fascinating and frightening to the male dreamer, who fears some loss of masculinity is prefigured. However, if it is explicable in terms of his relationship to his anima, then the pregnancy dream can be taken as a positive identification; he is 'pregnant' with possibility in terms of uniting his internal feminine with his masculine gender. It should also be remembered that true masculinity, or femininity, lies in such unity.

There is, of course, another simple and obvious explanation for male dreams of pregnancy. It may be a sympathy dream, if his wife or partner is pregnant.

What does it mean to dream of pregnancy if one is male? I had a dream that I was pregnant and I thought I was about 7 or 8 months. As I went out walking in the dream, I realised I was about 9 months! While walking, I felt my waters break and entered the hospital to have a Caesarean, in which I gave birth to a baby boy. I am a 33-year-old male.

Your dream greatly resembles dreams that are experienced by fathers-to-be! You don't mention whether this is your role. You may be close to a woman who is pregnant. This would go some way to explaining the dream. Another element of the dream could be related to your acceptance of the feminine part of yourself. This includes vulnerability, dependency, pregnancy, which are at odds with the stereotypical male image.

Male baby dreams usually follow the themes of creativity and birth or rebirth. They can also highlight very strongly an impulse (common to both male and female) to protect an entity that is weak and fragile.

This point is quite important. If dream babies point to birth, creativity and new beginnings, the symbol also embodies fragility and immaturity. It is essential to nurture and protect something that is precious but yet in its infancy: the baby, but also our nascent projects, creative undertakings and new beginnings.

As well as heralding external events, or changes in internal states that are reflected in profound external changes, dream babies can also indicate the infant Self. All the better if your baby is happy and healthy; but if the dream baby is sickly or inconsolable, the infant Self may be reliving past trauma. If the dream babies are troubling in this way, it usually indicates that such traumas are unresolved and deserve special attention. Or it may mean that you need to express some dissatisfaction about elements of your present life with the unmistakable force of a child's emotions.

Jung made a poignant comment on our adult relationship to children in his biography, *Memories, Dreams, Reflections.* He said that 'a characteristic of childhood is that, thanks to its naivete and unconsciousness, it sketches a more complete picture of the self, of the whole man in his pure individuality, than adulthood. Consequently, the sight of a child or a primitive will arouse certain longings in adult, civilised persons — longings which relate to the unfulfilled desires and needs of those parts of the personality which have been blotted out of the total picture in favour of the adopted persona' (1993, p. 272).

Our 'adopted persona' can trap us in rigidity and despair, doomed to self-consciousness. The idyllic antithesis — child-like wholeness — is symbolised in our dreams by the most powerful baby of all, the Divine Child. This archetype is present in most cultures in one form or another. For example, Christian iconography features the Divine Child as a cherub or angel. The ancient symbology of the alchemists featured the regally robed figure of the Divine Child to indicate the Philosopher's Stone — which represented identification with the eternal, and the god within. The Divine Child connects us with the part of ourselves that is not constrained by our persona or ego. The Divine Child may appear in dreams as vulnerable yet inviolable, reminder and guardian of our most precious hopes, aspirations, impulses and instincts.

4

Dream symbols and their meanings

I have cautioned you against looking for objective, literal meanings in the symbols that appear in your dreams. Every symbol has a particular organic relevance in the context of the dream, as well as a unique significance to the life of each individual. However, certain symbols (presented below in alphabetical order) appear very commonly in dreams that are sent to me, and I think it is very helpful to suggest possible interpretations. Remember that these interpretations are drawn from research into mythology, symbology, and considerable dream research; but they are interesting and apposite to the dreamer only when they coincide with the particular nature of the dream. Read them with interest, and they may offer you

Man also produces symbols unconsciously and spontaneously in the form of dreams.

– C.G. Jung
Man and His Symbols

strong 'leads' into your own psyche and the reasons why certain symbols occur. They may lead you to further reflection on the meanings of symbols as they occur to you in your dreams.

ANIMALS: Animals in dreams symbolise man's instinctual nature, energies and desires. If the animal is wild, then it is the untamed self that is highlighted; if a domestic animal is featured, then the symbolic untamed self is to some extent civilised. Animals represent the prerational instinct and the powers of the unconscious. Tribal societies identified strongly with animals in totems, rituals and sacrifices that celebrated and propitiated natural powers (see Aboriginal Dreaming on page 31). For civilised man, the animal is often a signal of a split from the forces of the unconscious. If the dream animal is dangerous, then the dreamer needs to readmit this force. As Jung said, 'Suppressed and wounded instincts are the dangers threatening civilised man; uninhibited drives are the dangers threatening primitive man. In both cases, the animal is alienated from its true nature; and for both, the acceptance of the animal soul is the condition for wholeness and a fully lived life' (1978, p. 266).

Children often dream of animals or monsters as an expression of their fears (see Nightmares on page 131).

If animals are appearing in your dreams, ask yourself what type of animal, what relationship you have to it, and note your emotional response. While an animal is often associated with fear, sometimes it brings with it a sense of exhilaration, reminding the dreamer of powerful unconscious forces that are subdued in daily life. Our language connects certain animals with similes that may be literally depicted in our dreams, for example greedy as a pig, strong as an ox, cunning as a fox.

Birds: Birds represent freedom, escape and movement in another dimension —

transcendence. Tribal shamans (holy men) donned bird masks to fly through the world. Birds are associated with the higher self and have spiritual connotations. Like angels, they indicate the soul, and the yearning for release from the physical plane (see Flying).

BLOOD: Blood symbolises completion, sacrifice. Blood is red, and blood is spilt; when flowing, it is allied with passions spent. It indicates that your 'sacrifice' or ordeal is over. The Arabic aphorism 'Blood has flowed, the danger is past' sums up the meaning of blood in a dream. For example, dreamers undergoing divorce may see an image of their ex-partner covered in blood. While this may be a profoundly disturbing symbol, it merely indicates that the marriage is over.

BOATS: Boats are linked through their association with water to the cradle, to the mother and to our earliest and most primal emotions. What emotions are you navigating and how?

CATS: Cats have always been associated with the female principle and, in Egyptian lore, with the moon. The black cat traditionally represents death and darker forces. The domestic cat, notable for both its cuddliness and its lofty independence, often makes an appearance in dreams. Ask yourself what the cat is telling you about your feminine, intuitive side, and the independent parts of your nature.

CHASED: Being chased in a dream is usually associated with fear. Ask yourself what or who is pursuing you. What pressure do you need to alleviate? Dreams of being chased are common in childhood, and often the pursuer is a monster or scary animal. In adult dreams, these motifs may continue, or the pursuer may be a personage, even the Shadow figure. The message is a strong one, and it is important to 'turn around' and face the fear. Dreamers who are able to do this (see Lucid dreams on page 121) report that they are able to confront and vanquish the pursuer once they examine the fear or pressure that it really represents.

CLIMBING: Sigmund Freud interpreted climbing as a longing for sexual fulfilment, but this image often carries connotations of aspiration in other areas of our life, such as personal or professional growth. Climbing motifs can include ladders, stairs, hills or mountains and elevators. How far up have you climbed? Are you afraid of falling or are you unable to climb further? Do you feel exhausted by the effort? Look carefully at the nature of the climbing motif to establish where you are in relation to your ambitions, and how you feel about them.

COLOURS: Colours can be associated with ambient emotional states — whatever you associate spontaneously with the colour dreamt about will usually be an indication of its symbolic significance. Especially strong, vivid colours often indicate the onset of a 'turning point' dream. *Black* is associated with the earth, darkness and the occult. *Blue* symbolises devotion and religious feeling, and innocence, and suggests the infinity of the sky. *Green* signifies fertility, abundance, sympathy and adaptability, and can also signify cycles of decay and regeneration. *Grey* is associated with ashes and can signify depression, inertia and indifference; it can also be associated with egotism. *Orange* is another religious colour, symbolising the dawning of spirituality, hope and new beginnings. *Pink* is the colour of the flesh; it symbolises love, emotions, vulnerability and sensuality. *Purple* is associated with power, regality and richness. *Red* signifies passion, sentiment, fire and blood; it is a vital, passionate colour also associated with sexual arousal, sensuality and even excess. *Violet* can indicate nostalgia and memories; it is often associated with water and thus the emotions. *Yellow* is associated with generosity, intuition and the intellect, and the warmth of the sun. *White* symbolises magic, purity, celestial bodies (the stars and the moon), caring and recovery.

CROSS-DRESSING: Dreams about cross-dressing may indicate hidden desires but are more likely to indicate an imbalance in regard to the gender-identification of the dreamer. Is your feminine/masculine side repressed or overactive? Are you disturbed by what your job or your associates require you to emphasise? How comfortable are you with the roles your gender imposes (see Dream Babies on page 62)?

DANCING: Dancing is closely linked to the act of creation. In tribal societies the oldest rituals of magic were performed in the dance. Dancing symbolises eternal energy. In dreams it is often joyful — the physical being achieving transcendence through movement.

DOGS: Dogs are noted for their loyalty and for being faithful guardians. It is for this reason that they are known as 'man's best friend'. They are the masculine intermediary between people and their instincts: they can hear and smell things that are not apparent to people. What is the dog doing in your dream? Is it leading you or accompanying you? Often the dog is associated with the animus in women's dreams. Here, the dog can manifest as aggressive and dangerous, expressing the unintegrated violence of the masculine principle (Hecate and the Hounds of Hell) in the feminine.

ELEPHANTS: Broadly speaking, elephants are associated with a sense of strength, wisdom and moderation. They are also associated with compassion and memory — the elephant never forgets. Is the elephant standing in for someone in your dream? Or does it represent a state of mind to which you aspire?

FALLING: Falling symbolises fear of failure or loss of power or control, for example 'falling in love'. Falling may indicate an overweening ambition, or suggest that the dreamer is living too much in the intellect and neglecting more basic aspects of physical and emotional well-being. Superstition has it that we will die if we hit the ground in a falling dream (probably because a great many dreamers wake up in shock before the point of impact). I can assure you that this is not the case! However, falling is a most unpleasant sensation and the shock of waking from it should be enough to ask yourself why your unconscious is sending you a message of this force (see Nightmares on page 131). Often the ground, or water, transforms itself at the point of impact in a dream of this nature. Dreamers rarely report distress; impact is often the starting point for a new segment of the dream. Ask yourself whether this variation of the falling dream is showing you something positive – that the fall you fear (from esteem, control, position) is not fatal. If the falling is related to a familiar site, then it may be worthwhile checking the area (for example, loose supports on a balcony or missing rungs on a ladder) because our subliminal conscious often picks up details that the eye does not see.

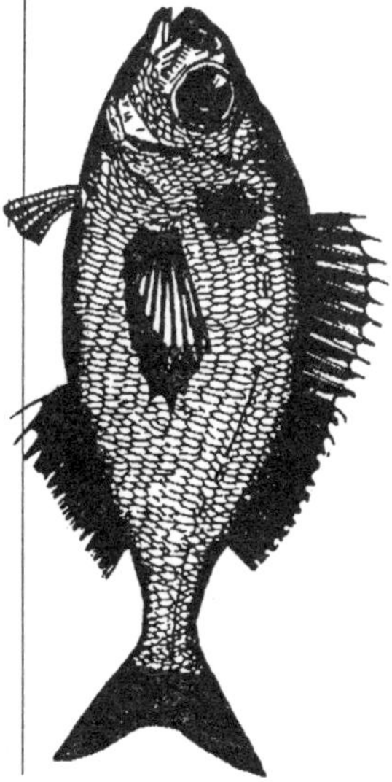

FISH: Being creatures of the water, fish are intimately connected with emotion, the life force and the unconscious. Water is the element of both dissolution and regeneration; the fish swims in water, the fount of all life, which gives this symbol a spiritual significance akin to that of a bird.

But, whereas the bird is related to the lofty spiritual plane, the fish is indicative of the spirit of the unconscious forces that are at the base of life itself. The association of the fish with Christianity has this primal spiritual symbolism at its core. Because they lay an extraordinary number of eggs, fish have been considered as a fertility symbol, often representative of sperm and male sexuality. In this way also, they represent spiritual abundance. The dream fisherman is a symbol of wisdom: the Fisher King, belonging to the legend of the Holy Grail, fishes symbolically in the depths of humanity's psyche to find spiritual enlightenment.

FLYING: Flying symbolises ambition, achievement, freedom. Often associated with a feeling of great joy, even ecstasy, flying usually indicates a positive feeling of power and transcendence (see Birds). Does this reflect your present situation or do you need to infuse some of this feeling into your waking existence?

Flying dreams are often experienced by people whose careers are highly visible to the public eye, such as media presenters and actors. This is because they have a subliminal need to stay 'on top'. Handicapped people also often report this dream: in this case, it offers a freedom and power at night that they are unable to enjoy during waking hours. Flying has also been associated with sexuality. Peak sexual experiences may induce a dream of high flight.

FOOD: Food symbolises nourishment. Why, how and what are you consuming? Are you hungry or have you eaten to excess in your dream? Are the images of food associated with guilt or pleasure? Eating is often connected with sexuality and sensuality: Freud suggests that fasting and gorging depict our sexual desires. Fasting can be related to self-punishment, whereas if you overeat in a dream it often represents greed or short-sighted grasping behaviour. Eating with others could indicate aspects of your social behaviour: if you feel uncomfortable, then this could be a sign of social awkwardness.

Are you having difficulties feeding from and giving to the relationships around you? Similarly, spoilt or bad-tasting food could relate to emotional nourishment, indicating problems in regard to a primary relationship. Fruits are traditionally recognised as obvious sexual symbols; chocolate signifies self-indulgence. Perhaps you need to indulge yourself more frequently.

GATES: The gate symbolises entry into a new world of opportunity and enlightenment. It may signify initiation into a higher plane of self-knowledge, and may suggest that the dreamer is now ready to attempt the next stage of an inner journey.

HORSES: Fleet and elegant, horses are powerful animals that have been tamed by humans for their purposes but always remain in essence wild creatures, subject to their instincts. Admired for its bravery and power, in dreams the horse relates to the power of instinctual, intuitive consciousness. Since ancient times, the horse has been associated with magic and divination, hence the talking horse of folklore and the lucky horseshoe. In mythology, the horse is associated with the wind, with the underworld, and with water. Riding a horse has often been associated with sexual intercourse. What message from your sources of intuition is the horse bringing to you? What power are you harnessing or ready to express?

Houses: Houses relate to the sense of self. The frontage of the house is significant: how is it presented? What is the image? Rooms within the house all have their own specific significance and it is important to note the state in which you find them and their importance within the rest of the dream house. Bedrooms are indicative of private, inner reality. The bathroom is a place of cleansing and release. The dining room is a place of formalised rituals, of eating and sustenance, while the kitchen is traditionally nourishing — the productive hearth and heart of the house. Foundations and floors suggest grounding and security; the ceiling and roof are about protection, but may also be about limitation.

If you are dreaming of stairs, note whether you are ascending or descending — are you exploring upper limits or grounding yourself? Walls refer to boundaries and partitions. What do you wish to integrate or to keep separate? Doors allow

movement between separated areas and relate spaces — in the dream state, inner spaces — to one another. Halls or corridors connect different areas of the house. Windows allow us to see out, or others to see in. How large are the windows? Are they heavily curtained or shuttered to hide the interior or shut out the exterior? Are they opened or closed? Large or small? Is your house cluttered with objects or sparsely furnished? Is it old or new, in a state of disrepair or well kept? How do you feel about your house?

The surroundings of the house are also important. Is the fence intact or broken? How does the garden grow? The house in your dreams is very important, reflecting your state at the time of the dream, or projecting essential information about hidden desires.

ISLANDS: Islands symbolise self-sufficiency and separation. The island in your dream may be expressing a need for peace and tranquillity away from the mainstream (or mainland); it may also indicate a sense of isolation.

JEWELLERY: Jewellery symbolises display, value and status. Are you wearing or coveting the jewels? Are you buying them for yourself, or is someone giving them to you? To dream of seeing a store window full of attractive but somehow unattainable goods often suggests the dreamer is excluded from the good things in life, but may also be a reminder to look elsewhere for more attainable and ultimately more worthwhile joys.

KEYS: Keys signify a solution to a problem, or access to understanding. What problem or issue are you on the verge of solving or resolving? Are you ready to accede to a new level of understanding? What areas are you ready to open up?

LIONS: Lions are associated with regality, courage, mastery, the sun and masculinity. Essentially, lions represent all the ruling animal passions. Are you endangered by devouring passions? What bravery are you showing or expected to show? The lion is strongly associated with the ruling aspects of the father (see Tigers).

LOVERS: There are several possibilities in a dream about a lover. It could be a wish for an ideal or particular person, or a need for sexual satisfaction. It could represent some quality missing in a relationship, or signify a need for tender, loving care, or it could relate to the anima/animus projection (see Anima/Animus on page 57).

MANDALAS: The mandala is one of the most mysterious and profound of the archetypes. The word 'mandala' means magic or ritual circle. It symbolises the state of wholeness to which the Self aspires. Often the circle is squared within or without, or contains four elements. The mandala is oriental in origin, although variations on the same shapes are found all over the world in all cultures. These variations include the wheel, the lotus flower, the rose, and in a dream, anything that appears as circular, or squared within a circular form. Often the circle and the square are juxtaposed with a triangle.

In oriental religions mandalas are used as a means of inducing meditation and assisting concentration. They encourage the spirit to move towards the Centre. However, mandalas have been used in all forms since the Paleolithic Age.

Many buildings — notably temples or sacred precincts — are designed on the principle of the mandala. In this case, the circle may not be the paramount shape, but the entirety of the ground plan radiates out from the central sacred space at the core.

Missing Things: Missing boats, trains or planes may indicate that you need to get ready for your future. Are you taking enough care of the everyday aspects of your life? Missing a station while travelling on a train or a bus can signify missed opportunities. What are you missing out on? The dream can be a strong pun, with the word 'missing' as the important element. Losing yourself or objects can indicate a loss of confidence or a sense of absence in yourself or your surrounding environment. You may have lost your direction in life, or be unsure of your next steps.

MOON: The Moon is associated with the tides and the physiological cycle of women. Because the Moon visibly changes through its own cycle, it has often been associated with biological change: growth to fullness to decline. In this way, it has always been taken as a planetary reflection of the human condition. In alchemy, the Moon was regarded as the guardian of the occult, in opposition to the Sun, which was signifier of the visible, physical world. The Moon has always been associated with volatility, femininity and the imagination, and the reflective qualities of thought.

MUSIC: Music is associated with creative talents and integration; it signifies the higher levels of inner development. Hearing music in dreams is quite rare, although when it occurs it usually conveys a strong message. If the music is harmonious, then creative potentials are being utilised; if discordant, then it may indicate that the creative force is distorted in some way.

NUDITY: Nudity signifies exposure and vulnerability. Are you afraid of being seen for who you really are? Often in the dream it is only the dreamer who is aware of nakedness. Note the tone of embarrassment, and where it appears in your waking life.

Paralysis: Experiencing paralysis in dreams indicates fear, anxiety and resistance to change. Are you in a rut? Do you have the sense of not being able to move forward in your activities? What habits are you unable to shift? In REM sleep, where most dreaming occurs, our motor functions are immobilised. This may be one reason for the image appearing. Heavy bedclothes have also been suggested, and some psychologists hold that continued dreams of paralysis point to the necessity of a change of diet.

Rainbow: The rainbow signifies hope and reconciliation, achievement and new beginnings.

Snakes: The snake is an exceptionally powerful symbol that hosts multiple meanings. A snake in a dream is usually remembered, because of our strong antipathetic associations with this reptile. It is most important to define your attitude to the snake, both in your waking life and in the dream, because this will give you the key to its particular significance. In Judeo-Christian belief the snake was the tempter that led to the Fall of Adam and Eve. It has long been associated with the power of the phallus; Freud makes much of this obvious connection with the male organ. In many mythologies, the snake represents pure, primal energy, but not always masculinity. In many Mediterranean cultures and in Egypt the snake was firmly associated with dualistic female deities (Persephone, Hecate) and vengeful female forces (the Medusa, whose hair was live snakes, and the Furies).

The multifaceted symbol of the snake has always included a good dose of evil due to its connection with primordial, reptilian energies. But once these forces are controlled, the snake has significance as a symbol of healing. In shedding its skin, it has come to be associated with regeneration. The two intertwined snakes on the staff of Mercury, which has become a symbol of medicine, represent the equal and opposite forces of the snake: its propensities to destroy and to heal. In Kundalini Yoga, the snake is a symbol of inner strength, which, living in the base of the spine, unfolds through all the energy centres of the body to the forehead, when man is able to recover his sense of the eternal. In ancient doctrines, the Ouroboros is the symbol of a snake biting its own tail:

thus underlining the essentially ambivalent but complementary nature of the snake, the life force wheeling through death and rebirth.

With this breadth of meaning, it is crucial to situate the snake in your dream very precisely in terms of dream landscape and your feelings. Does the snake represent some malevolent energy within either yourself or someone close to you? Does it relate to sexual energy? Is the snake representing a force that you have somehow neglected or overlooked? Look at your own negative emotions, or emotions that may be directed at you from those around you: jealousy, spite, vindictiveness, for example — all the emotions that can cause damage and feed on themselves. Are they a danger or is there some energy that can be transformed?

SPIDERS: A complex image, the spider has a dual significance. It spins a beautiful, fragile but fatal web, and places itself in the middle to ensnare and devour its prey. It is both endlessly creative and remorselessly destructive. To this extent, it has often been used to represent the duality of the natural law, and it also has associations with the Moon (waxing and waning) and a threatening Mother image. Most people are, to some extent, justifiably afraid of spiders. In dreams it may indicate someone untrustworthy in your vicinity; a plague of spiders may signify the pressure of too many responsibilities. Take careful note of your emotions in relation to dream spiders: they will give you clues about which elements of this symbols's dual nature your subconscious reflects.

TEETH: Teeth signify independence, communication and nourishment. Teeth falling out in a dream can signify impotence, fear of old age or deflated self-image. Make sure you have a dental check-up if this dream is recurring.

TELEPHONES: Telephones are associated with communicating indirectly or at a distance. What is the state of your intimate relationships? You may need to polish up your communication skills, in both your personal and your work relationships.

TESTS/EXAMS: Dreams of tests or exams indicate that you are experiencing some sort of ordeal or test in relation to your personal or professional life. It may be that you have set yourself or been given a task that stretches or is even above your abilities. Identify the ordeal to which your dream refers. Ask yourself if you have put enough time into preparation. Are you chronically afraid of failure? Does the dream reflect some trauma experienced at a time when examinations were a fundamental part of your progress? (Note that dreamers often relive a particular examination hall or location.) Is it that being in a position of authority worries you and gives you the image of being put to the test in your dreams?

TIGERS: Like the lion, the tiger represents animal passions that can either devour or create natural order. Also like the lion, the tiger is ruler of the jungle and at the apex of the natural hierachy. In Chinese mythology, the tiger represents both cruelty and darkness, as well as valour and protection. The dreamer needs to look to their passions and, possibly, to tame the tiger within (see Lions).

TOILETS: Urinating in your dreams represents a welcome release of emotional tension or anger. Sometimes, particularly in children, a urinating dream can result in wetting the bed. A urination dream may actually indicate that you need to go to the toilet; happily, for most adults, this results in awakening. Excrement is also linked with the elimination of processed emotional material. It has also been associated, paradoxically, with abundance in myth and folklore — embodying the moral that in what is most worthless we may find that of most value.

TRAVEL: Dreams about travel signify moving on to the next part of life's journey, progressing towards another personal or professional goal. Sigmund Freud suggested that travel and motion represent wishes for sexual fulfilment. However, it can be confidently said that

the journey is an archetypal image that refers to the seeking after knowledge, evolution and change. It is a symbol that has been used constantly in literature and art to depict the human condition of restless yearning towards fulfilment, and the process of individuation. Heroes always achieve their status in the process of a journey, where their mettle is tested and proven. Journeys can be a pilgrimage or a search. The scenery surrounding the journey may give clues as to the dreamer's internal state: is the scenery barren, arid, fertile, heavily populated, etc.? To travel is to aspire to an intensity of experience, to study new ways of being, to live with an energy and uncertainty that is not found in stasis. The journey, in dreams, is usually a quest: often for a spiritual centre, typified in legend as a Holy Grail. Dreams themselves are a journey through the internal landscapes of our unconscious desires, fears and aspirations.

VEHICLES: Dreams of cars, buses, trains, boats or other vehicles indicate how you are moving through your life. The *car* indicates your bodily Self and how you get around daily. If the car is broken down in the dream, it is worthwhile having it mechanically checked. Are you driving or are you being driven? If you are a passenger, then you are possibly at the mercy of someone else's power. Is the car going too fast or is it out of control? Slow down in your waking life. Are the brakes on? Is the car moving in reverse, or out of petrol? Whatever the state of motion of the car, it indicates how you are behaving in the process of your waking existence. The *train* is a vehicle over which we have no control, except to get on or off. It is also a vehicle on which we can rest and observe the landscape passing. What is the view from the window of the dream train? Where is the station? The *bus* is similar to the train, but associated with other passengers. What is your attitude in relation to others around you? The *boat* is linked through its association with water to the cradle, to the mother and to our earliest and most primal emotions. What emotions are you navigating and how?

VIOLENCE: Violence in a dream often appears at a distance, especially if the dreamer is committing the act or acts of violence. The emotional ambience may remain totally neutral and detached. This seems to imply that the dream's messages relate to conflict of another kind, like strong differences of opinion in the dreamer's mind, or some unresolved anger. When the dreamer is the victim of violence, then life conflicts are signalled. Do you have escalating debts? Is your health good? Are you in a threatening situation in any way at work or emotionally? Finding yourself in a war zone in your dreams depicts a need for reconciliation rather than victory over whatever you perceive to be represented by the 'enemy'. Of course, the enemy is within — it needs to be examined, and peace made. When the dreamer experiences self-violation, then this can represent guilt or a desire for self-punishment.

VOICES: Voices signify that you need to listen to your inner wisdom.

WATER: Water signifies the state of your emotions. It is strongly associated with unconscious depths, imagination and the source of creativity. It is also strongly connected to the mother and the womb, where we float in fluid before our birth. The nature of water is to be formless, yet powerful. It preserves and nurtures life. Baptism — meaning, symbolically, to be immersed or drowned so that one can be reborn in the life of the spirit — is an excellent metaphor for the primal necessity of dissolution in the unconscious to achieve higher levels of understanding, or true unity. Carefully note the type of water represented in your dream and think about how the nature of the water relates to your current emotional state. Is the water calm and unthreatening or flowing strongly, even flooding? Is the water frozen over, or is it a fountain, spurting forth vigorously? Is the water murky, with hidden depths, or swampy and fetid, or clear and sandy? Finally, where are you in relation to the water, and how do you feel about this? Are you swimming strongly, or just contemplating it before you?

Rain has a dual signification: water falling through air is strongly associated with rationality and intellect. Rain is also obviously associated with fertility, and with the higher elements nourishing the earth. The appearance of rain in your dream may signal the need to harmonise elements of your psyche, or may be a celebration that this is indeed occurring.

The *sea* is the primal water, the formless source from which all living things on earth emerged. For that reason, it has always been associated with the symbol of the Mother, and ante-natal life. *Drowning* is a powerful metaphor for being overcome by unconscious emotions. Often dreamers report that they feel as if they are drowning, only to discover that they can swim and survive in the watery dream element. Mothers often are very fearful after dreaming of a child drowning, but this usually indicates their subliminal knowledge that the child is ready to become independent. A *tidal wave* may indicate a deep fear of being overwhelmed by the emotions or circumstances surrounding the dreamer at the time.

WISE ELDER: The Wise Elder is an archetypal guiding figure of enlightenment or special power. It may be personified in a number of ways as a magician, witch or

sage, priest or any other authority figure. The Elder's presence indicates an initiation into a deeper meaning or higher consciousness, although the figures are not always benign and can often show a malevolent aspect. This often occurs when the figure is exhibiting projected fantasies of superiority and power; it may also simply indicate that the special wisdom being explored by the unconscious has the dual ability to be creative or destructive.

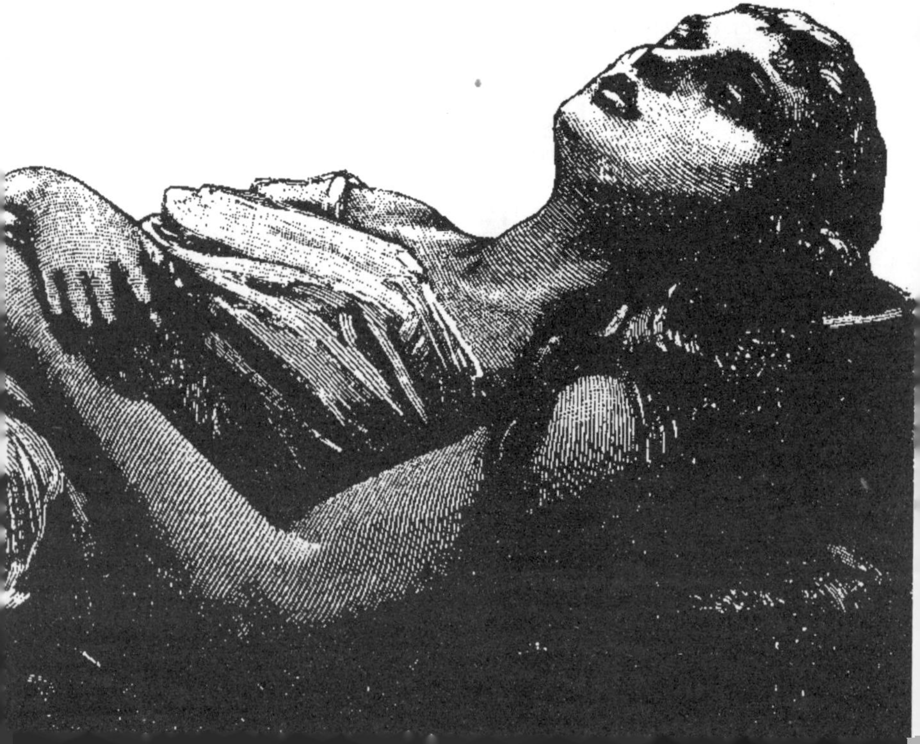

5

Common dream themes

PREMONITION DREAMS

There is no doubt that some people anticipate real events in their dreams. The examples are endless: from people seeing disasters such as car or aeroplane crashes that they are then able to avoid, to seeing themselves meeting people or taking part in events that subsequently happen. Sometimes the key is quite small but significant: a distinctive colour or object that is seen in the dream and then situates itself in a real-life occurrence.

Whether we call this type of dream a vision, a prophecy or a type of extrasensory perception (ESP) does not really matter. It appears to be an unconscious power that is experienced by many dreamers. Jung (and

Time present and

time past

Are both perhaps

present in time

future,

And time future

contained in time

past.

–T.S. Eliot,
'Burnt Norton'

many others) had distressing visions heralding the coming of the Second World War; Abraham Lincoln foresaw his own death. Constantine, Emperor of Rome, dreamt of winning his campaign under the sign of the cross. He subsequently converted to Christianity. Mohammed received the text of the Koran in a dream, and the Bible abounds in stories of the prophets' dream visions.

While history is full of examples of momentous premonitory dreams, such dreams can happen in everyday life to ordinary people. They can be about avoiding disaster, but they can also be about positive possibilities: starting a new business, meeting people, resolving a problem. It is these dreams that we will deal with in detail because these are far more common and fruitful. It must not be forgotten that for every truly premonitory dream of a disaster averted there are many disaster dreams which happily prove to be false alarms.

The mind relentlessly processes subliminal messages, even if most of these are not registered in consciousness. So the unconscious may 'know' things about the nature of the dreamer's environment that the conscious mind has not picked up. Hence, a dreamer may have a vision of being in a car with no brakes — and find, after checking the car, that the brakes have worn dangerously thin. A parent may dream of their child floating helplessly in the family swimming pool, and discover that the lock securing the pool gate has rusted and fallen off. These are obvious examples of our unconscious picking up details in our environment and alerting us before a crisis occurs.

There are the dreams in which a person who is present in our immediate environment behaves in an uncharacteristic manner, heralding, perhaps, a deception of some sort. Here, the unconscious is again alerting the dreamer that the Persona is not the only level on which people operate, and that there may be hidden agendas of which we are only subliminally aware but which may affect us adversely. Once again, our unconscious, dreaming mind is able to guide us for our own good.

Problems can often be solved in dreams. Examples of this have been well documented. Russian chemist Dimitri Mendeleyev solved the problem of constructing the periodic table, a problem with which he had been preoccupied for some time, as he dozed while listening to chamber music. He realised in a dream that the basic elements were related to each other like melodies. Many simple problems — whether to buy a house, take a trip or change a job — can also be solved in dreams. The popular advice 'sleep on it' expresses the ability of our dreaming minds to resolve troubling issues or pre-occupations during the night.

It also appears that the dreaming mind has the ability to move both backwards and forwards in time, and to defy conscious laws of space and place.

My son died 7 months ago of a drug overdose. An inquest is being held and is expected to conclude this month. A few nights ago, I dreamt that my son came home. Friends of his came to visit him including the one that had a baby boy 6 weeks after my son's death. There was a little girl in my dream, too, who called her father by his first name instead of calling him Dad. I then had a conversation with my son asking him why he died the way he did and he responded that he had just made a mistake. He was wearing black and looked well. A detective approached me with a photo, saying that the problem had happened when my son was three and a half, and the photo was a photo of our house at that time. He said that he was going to investigate the case and I was left feeling very satisfied with this information.

As you have been awaiting the outcome of the inquest your dream's message was one of reassurance and satisfaction. Your son appeared, as happens in visitation-type dreams, and the comments of the detective that the case would be sorted out are exactly in line with what you want to happen. Why not check back with the family regarding the house you were in at the time your son was three and a half? Do you remember any significant events that may have happened to him there? Generally, the feeling on awakening is the most important key to a dream, and as your feeling was one of satisfaction, then this is the emotion to hold onto.

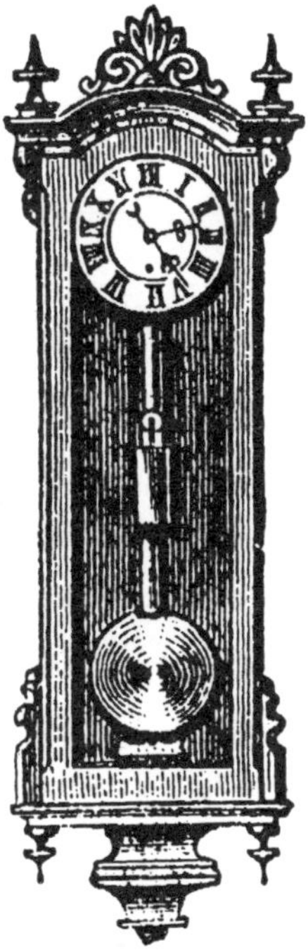

In this way, we are sometimes able to prevision events and people. In the case of events, it may be that the minutiae of our daily lives hold clues to what may come to pass, and that our unconscious processes these elements and predicts probable outcomes.

Dream visions of people we have not yet met are more difficult to fit to such an explanation, and may simply be evidence of the prophetic powers of the mind.

I would like to tell you about my dreams because a number of them have come true at a later date and some events happen the following day. The dreams that come true are more like visions. I will describe one of them to you. It was approximately 2 years ago, and at the time of the dream I was married, but we were having problems. I had a dream of a man whom I had never met. I couldn't see his face; I could see his clothes but his face was blacked out. My son was sitting between us and we were driving a ute. My son looked out of the window and said, 'There's my school'. I turned to the man and said, 'Remind me of my horse adjustment'. I did not own a horse at the time.

About 8 months ago my husband and I broke up and I started another relationship. My boyfriend, my son and I went for a drive one night. My son had started school just down the road from where I now live, and I had bought a horse just before I broke up with my husband. On this particular night we drove past the school and my son repeated what he said in the dream, although the dream was far from my mind. It was when I turned to my boyfriend and asked him to remind me of my horse adjustment that the memory of the dream returned. I looked at my boyfriend and said, 'Oh! It was you!' Of course, he didn't know what I was talking about. I have many occurrences like this and I don't always have to be asleep to experience these visions of the future.

Premonition dreams are reported by many dreamers, even when the subject matter is relatively insignificant. Your brain has the ability to run ahead and give you clear pictures of a happening in the future.

Visitation dreams — dreams in which relatives or close friends vividly appear (or reappear if they are dead) — are usually connected to a strong emotional bond. Often these dreams have an element of telepathy. Twins, for example, often report dreaming accurately of events happening to their other, even if they are not in contact at the time. Close relatives or family members may dream of each other, particularly if a warning of some sort, or a cry for help, is implied in the dream. In this case, the sense of distress felt by the dreamer usually impels an action which validates the contents of the dream.

Dreams of people who are dead may be equally distressing. To a large extent, they form part of the grieving process, allowing the dreamer to come to terms with loss. There may be a feeling of guilt involved: perhaps the dreamer did not have time to say 'goodbye' to the dead loved one, or held repressed resentment which was never aired. In these cases, and if the dream is persistent and troubling, I suggest the dreamer confronts the problem, and expiates the guilt by, for example, writing a

In my second pregnancy, I dreamt of an aura. In the aura I saw twin babies. I then took out a multiple birth insurance (early in the pregnancy). At 7 months I dreamt of twin boys. I gave birth to twin boys 2 months later. I collected on the multiple insurance. Weren't the twins lovely to let me know that they were two and not one? They certainly needed and used the money. Thank you to my twin sons.

This dream speaks for itself. The wonderful aspect of the dream is that the mother was listening to her inner self and took the message from her dream.

letter to the person in the dream, or visiting the gravesite. In any case, as with all recurrent dreams, it is most important to address the uncomfortable emotions that are dredged up.

I often dream of my brother, who was involved in an accident in 1991 and died. I dream of seeing him fit and healthy and he is smiling at me and very calm. I try to run to him but I am not moving anywhere. I often wake up crying after these dreams.

Recurring dreams of this nature depicting a visitation from a loved one who has died are dreams of reassurance. They can also relate to the period of grieving after death. The image of you being unable to reach him relates to a part of your own grieving process; when you understand this, the dream will not be so upsetting. Maybe you did not see him prior to the accident. This adds more weight to the visit in your dream. Try to accept these dreams as happy and positive, as your brother is, because they are messages from your subconscious telling you that your brother is still there to share feelings with, if not in body, then definitely in spirit.

I often hear reports of dreams in which a dead loved one issues a warning or conveys an urgent message. These sorts of dreams are quite common. Whichever way we look at them, they are usually quite important. It may be that we are able to receive messages from beyond the grave, or it may be that the dead loved one — due to a psychic charge associated with the emotional bond with the dreamer — comes to personify the part of the dreamer's Self that is able to intuit or telepathically project events. My advice to those who receive vivid messages or warnings of this sort is to heed them. It may be that the dream does not indicate an external state — an actual event about to happen — but rather an internal disequilibrium within the dreamer. However, the effect of being 'visited' is usually strong enough to state that something important is indicated, within or without.

The imagination may be compared to Adam's dream — he awoke and found it truth.

– JOHN KEATS, *LETTER TO BENJAMIN BAILEY 1817*

DAYDREAMS

Daydreams are not exactly dreams, although they belong to the same type of non-rational, non-directed thought. Usually defined as pleasant daytime reveries, daydreams have much to do with wish fulfilment and perhaps even with meditation. They are thought projections which often lead us to new ways of seeing; they are lateral and creative while also being unfocused and undemanding. It is important to distinguish obsessive, distracted thought, which can be stressful and morbid, and reduces concentration.

It seems to me that daydreams reflect what the dreamer may or may not be in real life. The subconscious, given a tranquil environment, projects to the daydreamer images of undeveloped potentialities or possibilities.

George Miller, one of Australia's eminent film directors, is eloquent on the fruitfulness of daydreaming. One of four children, all boys, he remembered that 'We never got bored. We used our imagination and when we had nothing to do we'd daydream, drifting away into the still dry air, the intense light and the heat haze to the sounds of the cicada and the cricket. Daydreaming was an okay thing to do — you weren't punished for it. Indeed, my career has come out of it because all my film ideas come through daydreaming!'

The key to daydreaming is to allow time. Many people daydream as a matter of course, particularly if they are in a creative field of work and have learnt the benefit of time-out for recharging the creative batteries. For those who want to tap into the benefits of daydreaming, make sure you allow yourself a gentle half-hour each day, in a quiet and restful place, and then just shut down. Allow the thoughts and images in your head to flow without interruption or direction, focusing only on pleasant images rather than on other preoccupations. Daydreaming, unlike sleep dreaming, really is about fantasy. Unlike sleep dreaming, you remain in control and conscious. Use daydreaming as a positive visualisation of what you would love to happen to you in your life.

EROTIC DREAMS

Sexual dreams are often well remembered for obvious reasons. Freud, with his theory of dreams as wish fulfilments, ascribed to most symbols a sexual meaning, but that is not what will be discussed here. Rather, the subject of this section is those dreams in which sex itself is portrayed in one form or another, and where the sexual act is actually felt or implied in the dream. Once again, it is essential to bear in mind that dreams, with their symbolic connotations, may use sex as a means of conveying a broader message.

Many of my readers write to me with dreams in which sex is explicitly depicted. These dreams make interesting reading! Many of them feature people who are not partners in real life. Often these dreams

The ruling Passion, be it what it will, The ruling Passion conquers Reason still.

– ALEXANDER POPE, *EPISTLE TO LORD BATHURST*

are pleasurable, but sometimes they are disconcerting; when violent sexual acts are played out, they can be extremely disturbing. In all cases it is important to interpret both the literal meaning and the symbolic meaning, which has wider connotations for the psychic life of the dreamer.

If you dream of someone for whom you harbour strong sexual attraction, then the dream is visioning a fairly straightforward fantasy. Whether or not it is appropriate for you to imagine sex with this person is another issue. In any case, repressing strong desire is a sure way of creating a dangerous tension, and the dream may be alerting you to this fact. It is important to remember that sex in dreams is not sex in real life. Attraction to others is a part of life, and repressing this will not help. If you have developed a strong lust for your neighbour's wife or the grocery man it may be that you need to put it in perspective, or that you need to look at the reality of the situation. If you are in a monogamous relationship and your dreams are merely mirroring a conscious attraction, then you may need to have a long, hard look at your primary relationship. Does the dream lover represent something that you are not receiving or giving? Is it time to re-evaluate? Do you actually know the neighbour's wife or grocery man well, or are you projecting unconscious and dream-heightened fantasies?

Often, dreamers in a perfectly harmonious relationship will enjoy erotic dreams featuring someone they know, but to whom they are not consciously attracted. In this case, it may be a simple acknowledgment of the fact that the dream partner may turn the dreamer on, in some subliminal way, or that the dream partner has a special quality that may be appealing. Both of these viewpoints are not particularly threatening. It does not for a moment mean that the primary relationship is in danger, although it may be worthwhile examining the dream to find out if it indicates the existence of an area that needs some work. What is it about the dream partner that is so attractive? In what situation did you find yourself?

Similarly, dreamers will often enjoy sexual encounters with movie stars or celebrities. In this case, the illustrious dream partner usually holds a conscious significance for the dreamer. It may be that they embody characteristics that the dreamer finds expecially attractive, erotic or just downright sexy. We are confronted daily with images of delicious beings who strut their stuff through our various media. Only a hermit would fail to be affected! There's not much point in worrying too much about a pleasurable dream of this nature. Just lie back and enjoy — after all, it's most unlikely that the dream star will affect your real life! Once again, the dream may simply point to areas that are lacking in your own life. It simply may be that you are looking for a little extra excitement.

It is important to remember that during REM sleep our sexual organs are showing all the signs of stimulation, even if we are not dreaming about sex. In adolescence, sexual dreams may result in 'wet dreams' in men and orgasm in women. A period of enforced abstinence may result in sexual dreams. These are all straightforward physical reasons for sexual dreams which need little analysis.

Some dreamers are shocked to find that they are having intercourse with fathers, brothers, mothers, sisters or other relatives, or engaging in sado-masochistic behaviour, prostitution or other forms of sexuality that they would not 'dream' of pursuing in their conscious sexual lives. These dreams need a bit more work, because they may be indicating significant areas of concern in intimate relationships. By this I do not mean that the dreamer is in danger of turning into a deviant. I mean that sex itself is a potent symbol of intimacy and of power. These dreams have a metaphorical significance that is unequivocally depicted in the sexual act.

Similarly, dreamers often report feeling disturbed on waking from a dream in which they are enjoying intercourse with someone of the same sex. Contentedly homosexual dreamers may discover that they are dreaming of intercourse with someone of the opposite sex. If we bear in mind the symbolic significance of the sexual act, and remember the significance of the Shadow and the Anima/Animus (see chapter three), we can put this sort of dream into perspective. It may be that these dreamers need to engage more fully with their own feminine or masculine power, or with the power of their internal opposite.

Another characteristic of sex is that, ideally, it leads to physical climax. It gratifies a primary urge, like the need to eat or drink. Sexual dreams depicting frustrated intercourse may point to areas in the dreamer's daily life that are profoundly unsatisfactory and frustrating, or to a need to be released from a constrictive situation.

When I was younger I was sexually abused. In a recent dream it was happening again, but the face of someone I trust who appeared in the dream was completely taken over by the abuser, then switched back and forth. I felt hatred for my friend. Can you please tell me why I see him as the abuser for it is bothering both of us.

I trust you received counselling for this abuse of the past. If you didn't you most definitely should. Your dream contains shifting imagery from your memories to the present, and it is connected to the now of your life as sexuality demanding to be recognised.

They may also indicate a deep fear of failure or impotence in relationships.

Rape or sexual abuse is deeply distressing in real life and in dreams. Dreams of this nature may refer to an event in the dreamer's past. In this case, professional help should be sought immediately. Having suffered the abuse is bad enough in the first instance; it should not have to be relived night after night in dreams. Counselling will alleviate the psychic scars by allowing the unconscious to release the trauma.

Dream events of this nature, when not referring to an actual event, are symbolic of a significant power imbalance. It is essential to decode the dream and examine the contents to properly attribute where these imbalances lie.

Dreaming of an ex-lover or ex-spouse may indicate that unresolved issues hanging over from that relationship are presently at play in the dreamer's waking life. There may be similar circumstances unfolding in the current primary relationship or marriage, or in another relationship that somehow acts as a mirror. It is therefore very important to examine the dream in the light of the former relationship, and then to connect it to your present situation.

In my dream I start off by taking two or three strides then launch myself into the air. I then glide slowly above the ground at a level of about 50 feet, with my arms usually in the crucifix position. Hand movements control flight direction and altitude. The location of these flights varies but it is always to a place I have been before, sometimes many years ago. The people in the dream are not in any way familiar, and they seem to regard my floating as nothing unusual, sometimes smiling and waving. I then leave the area but I am now flying at great speed. I always head towards a mountain (shrouded in very dark clouds). This mountain is shaped like Japan's Mt Fuji. Just after I enter the clouds I feel intensely cold. I then wake up shivering.

Your experience in this dream is related to your sexuality and the fact that you cannot bear the thought of losing control. Flying signifies ambition and sexual prowess as well as a sense of freedom. The feeling of great speed and flying towards a mountain is a description of you reaching your peak. When you felt the cold and shivering this is associated with your exaltation and the solitude of your dream experience.

I had a dream that my husband and I were at a motel with two of our friends who are also married. There was a swimming pool at the motel and my friend's husband was lying down on a lazy boy at the far end of the pool. I dived in and swam to the end and then got out and sat next to him. We were talking and then all of a sudden we started to kiss passionately. It was such a beautiful feeling and we were just about to sneak to a room and I woke up. I can't stop thinking of this dream but I don't understand it as I love my husband very much.

The location of your dream is suggestive and the fact that you dived into the water to reach him depicts your emotions and how you will achieve whatever you desire. It could be that you need reassurance from your husband that he would do the same for you. Often the dream's message is in reverse. Your husband may be in need of some attention — or is it you? Put TLC on your shopping list!

I had a dream which was quite horrifying and embarrassing in retrospect, though not at the time of dreaming. I dreamt I was inserting a branch of a rose bush, about 10 inches long and covered in thorns, into my vagina, while my father looked on from a few metres away. My father had a beard and was young in this dream (which is not the case in reality). He had a vaguely quizzical look on his face as I carried out this bizarre procedure, as if to ask, 'Doesn't that hurt?' I was aware it might hurt as I pulled the branch out so I removed it with care.

It is interesting to note that you weren't embarrassed during the dream — only when you realised what the images portrayed. As well as being the traditional symbol for love, the rose has often been said (by Freud most notably) to signify female genitalia or the blood of menstruation. Depending on what time of your life this dream occurred, I would say your sexual development and indeed your sexuality was focused on your father. It is common for little girls of any age to imagine their father as their lover. In this case he was an observer of an intimate act. If this dream happened prior to your first sexual encounter then I am sure you can understand its message.

Not so long ago I dreamt that I was having a shower when my older brother came into the bathroom and the water turned so hot that it burnt me. He then pulled me out of the shower, threw me on the floor and began raping me. The bathroom door was open a bit and I could see my parents in the next room so I started screaming out for them to help me — but they didn't! I have had this and similar dreams quite a few times.
What do they mean?

Sibling rivalry is one of the reasons behind a dream like this. You saw yourself as the victim in a dream at a time when your sexuality is defining itself. Rape in a dream can signify that you have been taken advantage of in some other area of your life.

The most telling part of your dream is your attempt to get your parents to help you in the face of your brother's power and dominance, and their lack of response. It may be a good idea to talk to them about this.

Your dream shows that you are experiencing a natural stage of development.

Recently I dreamt I was going to a friend's house. I arrived and went into the garage and was suddenly surrounded by a group of men in their fifties, who wore old army uniforms and crazed looks on their faces. They moved in and I was raped. Afterwards my boyfriend turned up and was happy and laughing. I wanted to tell him what they had done but I couldn't speak. I ran outside to my car but it was gone. I was terrified, so I just ran. I woke up feeling very sick. What could this mean?

Your dream is filled with the symbolism of vulnerability and frustration. Are you in a situation at work where you have to fight your superiors for recognition? The vulnerable side of you makes you the victim in your dream. Frustration and anxiety show up in your inability to speak and in the loss of your car when you especially needed it. The car often represents our physical energy and how we 'drive' through life. It seems as though something in your life is blocked and timid, and you need to release it.

I am 19 years old and have had a very distressing dream. I don't know the whereabouts of the dream but I am confronted by an older man and threatened with rape. I tell this man he would have to kill me. I then wake up in a hospital bed with my father watching over me. I go to talk but cannot. This is due to my throat being slashed and bandaged up. I later find out that I have been raped, and have the urge to end my life with the help of my father. That's as far as it goes, but I would like to add that I feel funny around older men, quite uncomfortable. What does this mean?

Your experience in your dream makes me think that you may have suffered sexual abuse as a child. If this is not the case, then something important is shifting in your life. Are you leaving home? Maybe it is time for you to step out on your own and without your father's aid, you don't feel capable. Hence the dramatic messages in your dream. Our dreams sometimes shock us so we remember them. This could be your message. You may be suffering doubts about your sexuality and it seems your father is the key to this. You need to discover more about your own sense of self, to build up a stronger sense of self-esteem.

Recently I have been having vivid dreams of watching my boyfriend make love to a woman I know. The dream started with both of us running our hands over his naked body. She then proceeded to make love to him. I can only describe the feeling as unbearable; it was like having someone die who was very close. The scary part was that I felt as if I deserved it. Afterwards I took the woman home and was very nice to her, but on returning to my boyfriend, I informed him I would not sleep with him for 3 months until he had an AIDS test. What could this mean? He is a wonderful man who would never cheat on me. We are both firm believers in our relationship. I have also been having dreams about being married to a horrible man, but at the same time having an affair with my current boyfriend. I love him very much, and to have such vivid dreams really scares me. I cannot look the woman from the first dream in the eye anymore. Please help!

In real life it sounds as if your relationship is one of the 'perfect' kind, yet in your dreams you act out an opposite role. Your boyfriend was almost like the plaything of you and your female friend. Perhaps she has shown him attention or affection in real life? This sort of dream image often coincides with this sort of real-life situation. In both of your dreams you appear to be the instigator of the problem, and he becomes the vulnerable and unwitting partner. I wonder if you indulge in self-punishment fantasies? There is the sense of victim hanging over these dreams, so you should watch for this in waking life.

LUCID DREAMS

Lucid dreaming has been a controversial topic for some time, but there is really no longer any doubt that it is a perfectly natural and frequent phenomenon that occurs spontaneously. The process is quite simple: a lucid dream is one where the dreamer is aware he or she is dreaming, and can, to a greater or lesser extent, control what happens in the dream. Most prolific dreamers have experienced lucid dreams. The greater challenge is to exert control over the events and symbols of the dream. But why should this be important?

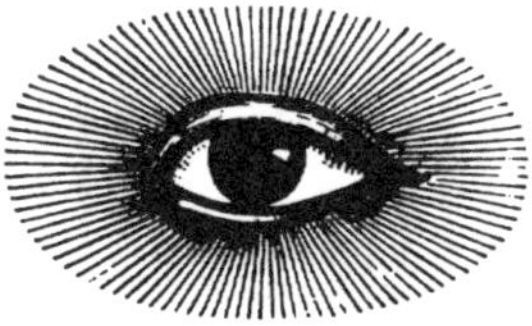

Our truest life is when we are in dreams awake ...

– HENRY DAVID THOREAU

My friend was in bed asleep and he had a nighmare in which something pulled his finger. He woke up terrified. It took him about half an hour to get back to sleep. When he did, he had the same dream again, so he pulled 'its' finger back, then woke up feeling really good.

This reaction by your friend is great! It is exactly what we should all try to do when frightened by something or someone in a dream or nightmare.

Apart from the fact that some may find this a stimulating night-time hobby, lucid dreaming can heighten the awareness of the messages and images that the unconscious is formulating in the dream. So, by becoming 'conscious' during our nocturnal journeys, the integration of dreaming with waking life is facilitated to a greater degree than it would otherwise.

Lucidity brings with it some degree of control over the outcomes of the dream. Practice can contribute to the ability to achieve this. At the very least, lucid dreamers can choose how they wish to respond to their dreams. For example, if encountering an ominous dream figure, the dreamer may decide to confront and examine its nature. Similarly, a joyful dream experience can be relished and prolonged. This is possible only if the dreamer is aware that he or she is dreaming. In this way, it is possible for the dream to become a sort of therapy: unconscious messages are filtered through what I will call the sleeping consciousness and can be comprehended with less equivocation.

In short, by according consciousness more power while we sleep and dream, we accord the unconscious a more powerful role in our conscious (waking) lives. If we accept that harmony between inner and outer states is a desirable human goal, then lucid dreaming is a useful aid for integration.

One of the world's leading exponents of lucid dreaming, Dr Stephen LaBerge (1990), has charted many ways to achieve lucidity in dreams. These include variations on Tibetan yogic techniques, as well as techniques he and other modern researchers have developed through rigorous experimentation. The broad thrust of the techniques is to encourage recognition of oneself in the dream state. Other techniques involve stimulating the mental conditions for lucid dreaming before sleep, methods of entering sleep and developing special sleep patterns.

The most important step is the first one: developing your sense of dream recall and dream awareness. LaBerge then goes on to recommend 'reality testing': assessing the environment to test whether you are asleep or awake. Reality testing can be practised during waking hours. When testing while in a dream, the dreamer will notice things out of place or shifting or surreal in some way. This identifies the dream state. The dreamer can then work on exploring the dream, in which he or she is aware.

When I was younger I used to have recurring nightmare that I would walk into our bathroom and there would be a hand and a forearm coming out of the wall. I would pull it and it would come off and I would scream. One night when I pulled, a clown fell out, and I haven't had the dream since. Does this mean I have gotten over the fear that I had? I am 21 years old now.

Yes, you have confronted your fear in your dreams. There is no need for you to fear a clown!

In my dreams I travel to places a lot, like astro-travel! My dreams have a beginning, a middle and an end. If I wake up before the ending happens, I'll dream the ending the next night. Every so often I go back to visit people and places. These dreams are always in colour and I can remember them in vivid detail for months. I can't explain them. Astro-travel could be possible. The dreams are never bad or upsetting.

It seems you are experiencing a type of lucid dreaming, where you make desires come true. It is a different type of consciousness, and one your mind obviously enjoys and has worked out with some degree of sophistication. Maybe it is possible to include some of your destinations in your everyday life. Try to make your dreams come true!

I recently had a dream but still to this day I'm sure I was awake. One night I was trying to go to sleep, and when I closed my eyes something strange happened. I felt a little nauseous, so I opened my eyes only to find myself rising off the bed. I felt I was about 1 metre in the air. It frightened me so I closed my eyes again, and started to spin, first one way and then the other. Then I floated back down to the bed. My house was quiet and normal, and there was nothing unusual in my room. Eventually I went back to sleep. I have never had this experience again and hope I never will; it was most upsetting and scary.

To have felt upset or frightened by your experience is the clue to what the dream means to you. Sensing your physical body floating is the prelude to a new type of consciousness developing from within. This can be related to erotic flying dreams and can correspond to the feeling of a special high that comes when we let natural energies flow. Your fear may come from a lack of knowledge about your own instincts, or just the fact that you had no control over the situation. I think you were lucid-dreaming, but did not know how to direct your dream. If it happens again, remember that it is possible to do this. In the meantime, try to accept any new changes you are sensing from your inner self. Don't fight them; learn to grow with them.

RECURRING DREAMS

When a troubling dream returns to us over and over again, it indicates that the message is not being interpreted or confronted adequately by the dreamer. I am often asked to comment on dreams that have plagued the dreamer from their childhood until late into adult life.

Generally speaking, a dream of this kind is usually an attempt to compensate for a blind spot in the dreamer's attitude to life, or it may date back to a traumatic moment or event that has been left unresolved in the unconscious.

For the past 20 years I have been having a recurring dream about big cats. These cats are lions, tigers, panthers and cheetahs. In my dream they are always attacking me and just as I am about to be killed I wake up in a terrible sweat.

The animals in your dreams symbolise your instincts. How do you view these animals in real life? As your dream has been recurring over such a long period, there could be one or two reasons for this. First, you could have got into a rut with this dream, and expect it to return now and then. Try to remember when it began. The dream could relate to an incident that occurred at a particular time of your life. It may pop up like an anniversary to remind you of the past. Second, these cats are of the untamed variety. Something about your wilder instincts is being repressed, or you may be fearful of the expression of these instincts in another.

One dreamer who approached me for guidance was an elderly woman who had, since childhood, experienced a recurring dream of herself lost in a wide, dark place. She identified this place as a forest. After I talked with her about the dream, she remembered that she had been lost and terrified in a park near her home as a little girl.

Another dreamer was troubled by a vision of herself as a young girl of about 6 years old, standing awkwardly in a white dress with a large bloodstain on the front at the level of her hips. After discussion, she realised this image related to an incident of abuse which happened to her at about that age. It was significant that the little girl, her invaded child-self, appeared to her at times when relationships were beginning or ending – times of great vulnerability.

Frequently, after we examine and accept the emotional difficulty symbolised in the recurring dream, it ceases to recur.

Dreamers often report that the recurring dream is exactly the same each time it is dreamt; however, on closer examination, this is rare. Most commonly, a recurring sequence or significant symbol will occur in the wider context of a dream. If you are subject to a recurring dream, try to note down all the details each time it occurs. You may notice a progression or development in the nature of the symbols presented or the context in which they arise. This will give you a chance to reflect on where you stand in relation to the dream, psychically, each time it reappears.

I always have dreams about being on a surfboard on the ocean and being attacked by sharks. I always seem to get in to the shore somehow. These dreams puzzle me because I love the sea. What can they mean?

You may love the sea, but if you are a surfer then your fears have at least a possible basis in reality. Being attacked in the ocean by a creature from the deep indicates you are feeling emotionally attacked. Ask yourself, what do sharks mean to you? As this is a recurring dream and you are subconsciously attuned to its recurrence, consciously visualise yourself fighting back. This may change the course of the dream next time you have it. Remember that the shark is a predator and you must be wary of anyone in real life who may have predatory designs.

I have a recurring dream that I am in an elevator by myself. I push a button to go to the fortieth floor; the elevator takes off like a rocket, and I can hardly hang on. When I get to the top, I step out and have a look, get back in and push the button for the ground floor. Again the lift takes off like a rocket and I can't hang on. My head keeps hitting the top of the elevator.

You are certainly experiencing some highs and lows! Is this happening in your everyday life? Can't you get it together? Examine your personal life or career; a strong desire is being depicted, but then returning to the ground. Dreams of out-of-control elevators are similar to dreams of falling. Who or what is in control, and why?

In my recurring dream my younger child is always head-down in water, either a pool, a river or a beach. When I find her and lift her out of the water she is always alive. This dream disturbs me greatly.

This type of dream is prevalent among mothers with young, growing children. Seeing a child drowning in a dream may reflect your fears about her stage of growth or independence. Death in dreams is really the ending of a stage, or completion. It is not necessarily death in actuality. Look back on your own life and try to remember if a similar situation occurred to you or your siblings. If you cannot swim, this could be a reason for the dread you feel. Naturally, security precautions should be a top priority if you have a pool.

Sometimes, the recurring dream holds a less painful import. Some are purely joyful, like some flying dreams. The dream can signal to the dreamer their particular state of mind in relation to an ongoing psychological issue. Most dreamers have their own unique dream signs — signature motifs that recur frequently in different dream narratives to indicate how things are faring in their conscious lives. One dreamer was visited by horses. They were never the same colour or size, but after some time she came to realise that they signalled to her the state and energy of her creative powers at any particular time. For the most part, she welcomed their presence as vigilant messengers from her unconscious.

I have recurring dreams about dolphins and water. In one of these dreams I was actually staring into a dolphin's eyes and swimming with it.

Dolphins are swift and gentle and also known for their friendliness to people. As the ocean often represents the unknown of our emotions, your experience with the dolphin shows you quite comfortable in this medium. This is a very pleasant dream and one you should simply enjoy.

Another function of the recurring dream is to prefigure an event of great significance. Jung had a dream for many years which signified his quest for and integration of ancient alchemical lore into his theories. He foresaw, in the last of his dreams of this sequence, symbolic illustrations that were to appear in reality in a sixteenth-century alchemical text he obtained some weeks later. From this point on, the dreams ceased.

NIGHTMARES

Nightmares fall into three categories:

- the 'classic' nightmare, from which the dreamer awakes with a start as he or she succumbs to whatever horror is envisioned;
- the 'bad dream', where frightening, sad, angry or unpleasant images appear in a dream narrative but do not force the dreamer awake;
- the night terror, most often suffered by children between the ages of 3 and 8 years, but sometimes also by adults, from which most dreamers awake without any recall of the elements of the dream.

All nightmarish dreams have in common a heightened level of anxiety.

There are common motifs that occur during these dream episodes: savage animals, monsters, falling, drowning, being chased, crushed, bitten, stabbed. Of these — which are but a handful — the many permutations of violence and threat are specific to the dreamer.

It is interesting to note that up until the development of the concept of the unconscious in the late nineteenth century, nightmares were thought to embody 'real' visitations of demons and succubi (female demons reputed to have sexual intercourse with men in their sleep). In fact, the term 'nightmare' actually means 'night demon'. Myth and fairytale are peopled with such demonic, magical figures, thought to torment the helpless individual. However, in these stories the battle with such monsters usually follows a formula that gives us a vital clue: the beast is usually defeated once it is confronted and faced down or attacked, and with the defeat comes transformation.

With the refining of depth psychology, we have come to see that nightmares in all their forms, except perhaps night terrors, actually reflect internal psychic conflicts. The disturbing power of the nightmare lies in its forceful indication of the extent of the discord. But, as in myth, once the beast within is confronted and/or vanquished, real integration and transformation can proceed.

The classic nightmare is related to deep-seated fears and frustrations. Nightmares are not common occurrences in an average dream life, but when they arise it is important to take careful note. The nightmare can be most unpleasant to experience, which is one of the reasons why we remember it so vividly, but examining it can be extraordinarily fruitful for the dreamer. It is in the land of nightmare that the most fearful monsters, difficult situations, and deepest resentments are found. Nightmares that are clearly linked to a daytime incident usually indicate that something in the incident tips

off a deep emotional response, perhaps in an area that the dreamer hides even from himself. The more 'thin-skinned' the dreamer, the more likely they are to suffer from nightmares, simply by virtue of their heightened experience of emotional states.

This is not to say that having nightmares indicates the presence of a terrible neurosis or psychosis. It can simply be a pointer to essential human concerns and drives: survival, nurturing, love, rage, esteem, family, work. Or it can relate to a personal vulnerability or problem that keeps cropping up in the normal course of life. It would be a very rare being who did not harbour a whole set of weaknesses and fears and the denial mechanisms that go with them. Nightmares are revealing. They tell us how well we are coping in this uncomfortable region of the psyche. They are also reminders that the Persona is only a well-structured interface that allows us to operate in the world. The monsters of the deep are beneath; they are an essential element of being human.

Consequently, it is very important to decode the nightmare and to chart the psychic territory it reveals. Often the Shadow is present, or some other imaginative fiend. Often the dreamer has travelled in the nightmare landscape before,

From ghoulies and
ghosties and long
leggetty beasts
And things that go
bump in the night,
Good Lord,
deliver us!

– CORNISH PRAYER

because nightmares are commonly recurring (although sometimes not frequently) until the dreamer resolves the issue at hand.

It is in this context that I will mention post-traumatic stress disorder nightmares. Soldiers who have seen combat at close hand, for example, may often take years to 'debrief', and may find that other stressful incidents in their subsequent lives trigger these nightmares. Abuse victims may assiduously bury their pain, and relive it under the guise of a horrific nightmare, time after time.

Other causes of nightmares are certain medications (see your doctor if nightmares escalate after being prescribed drugs), overindulgence in alcohol, and some physical conditions like high fever (see chapter six).

Night terrors occur in a deep-sleep phase of the night, not during REM sleep, which may explain why they are not remembered but instead leave only the unmistakable emotional and physical residue of extreme fear.

While having a spectacular effect on the victim, night terrors are the least understood sort of nightmare. They appear to be hereditary to a certain degree, and are most prevalent in children. Environmental or emotional factors also appear to

I am a horror movie fanatic and I recently saw The Exorcist. *Afterwards, I had a nightmare where I heard voices telling me to look behind the door. When I did I saw myself burning in hell; a white light flashed and then I woke up!*

Seeing horror movies encourages you to dream of horrid things. You succeed in terrifying yourself and perhaps this is a lesson to you *not* to watch them before bedtime, if you must at all!

play a part in their occurrence. Adults who suffer from night terrors usually have this sort of dream episode in the first couple of hours of sleep and often when they are extremely stressed or fatigued. Often they do not remember anything except fragments. Once again, drugs or medical disorders may be a contributing factor. Night terrors are distinguishable from other nightmares by certain factors: the sleeper will awake in a highly agitated state, but will be incoherent and completely disorientated. Children do not recognise their parents in this phase. Gradually they will calm, and will usually awake the next morning without remembering any detail of the episode.

I had a terrifying recurring nightmare throughout my childhood years and I can still remember it vividly now. There was a fast-flowing wide river going downhill; a gaily coloured flat-bottomed boat (like a barge) was travelling downstream in the flow of the water. The canopy was striped in bright colours and made a roof over the boat. In the boat was a skeleton, dripping blood, and crocodiles were rising out of the water ripping at it. I appeared to be above the scene looking down on it all; I seemed not to be upset at what I was looking at. The reason I ask about this dream is that for the first time in my life (I am 33 years old) I am living without addicted persons (family members) close to me. I need help to fill in the grey areas from my childhood.

The flowing river probably indicates your desire to explore the unknown reaches of your emotions. I feel the skeleton is associated with your personality and that you must have had to sacrifice much of yourself to survive the voracious crocodiles. Could this mean your family? Was floating above it all the only way to deal with it?

I am hoping that you will find some time to help me to understand a horrific dream I had several weeks ago. This dream seems to have ignited a whole series of nightmares that plague me almost every night to the point where I am frightened to close my eyes. My insomnia is affecting my husband and my marriage, so I desperately need some answers. We live in a three-bedroom fibro-tile home. It is our first, purchased only a few months ago. I have been married for 2 years and we have a 12-month-old boy. The dream occurred on a Friday morning at approximately 1 a.m.

My dream takes place in our home. I am alone with our son. In my dream I also have a newborn girl asleep in a bassinet in one of the rooms. It is late afternoon and I am expecting my husband home from work at any moment. The house is familiar on the inside but from outside it is much older and much like an old Federation home with very high foundations. I am holding my son and looking out the front window for any sign of my husband, as the weather is taking a bad turn. I then notice that there is a woman staring at me from the window of the house across the street. This frightens me (I have never met the people across the street). A few minutes later the doorbell rings. It is the woman, who is in her thirties and attractive. She says she has been watching me for a long time, and warns me of some sort of danger, telling me to be careful. She then seduces me; I become aroused and we engage in foreplay. We stop abruptly; she leaves without saying a word and resumes her position in the window across the street. I watch from behind my screen door as the wind becomes wild and a storm is coming. At that moment my husband pulls up in the driveway and I run to him excitedly, telling him of the day's events, but he doesn't listen. He takes me by the hand and leads me to the side of the house, telling me he found something under the foundations he wants to show me.

When I look all I can see is some junk and old furniture. I follow my husband under the house, holding my son in my arms when suddenly something catches my eye. Hanging on a coathanger in the dark, billowing with the wind, are priest's garments — red with a white lace pinafore. I scream and Jim comes running. I have no idea how it got there or what it is doing there. The garments are clean and pressed. The fact that they are so misplaced scares me to death. I run out; it is almost dark, the wind is slamming all the doors in the house and I have to go and check on my little girl. Then I stop in my tracks. The earth in front of my feet is beginning to break open, and from it rises an old skull and crossbones draped in a black cloth. I scream, and with tears streaming down my face, tear into the house. It is dark except for the lightning. The curtains are flying, doors are banging and there in the middle of the hall, towering over me, stands a woman in black, with long, ratty black hair, a ghost-white face, red mouth, pointing long fingers in my face and screaming 'Get out!'.

I found myself screaming in my sleep. My husband was shaking me, and I had goosebumps from head to toe. My heart was beating so hard I thought I was going to have a heart attack. The dream was so vivid it took me a few days to shake myself back to reality. No dream has ever affected me like this before. I did not watch any horror movies that week and can't seem to find any explanation for it. My mother-in-law thinks I should have the house blessed and consequently I am having a priest come over this weekend to do just that. Since that night I have had many different nightmares. Can you please help?

I feel you should definitely look into what has gone on in this new house of yours prior to your arrival. If you are not receiving any medication of any kind then I am sure you should not be experiencing such a horrific nightmare. Without speaking to you further about the details of your life and your past, it is very difficult for me to be more specific. The images seem very vivid and detailed, and may relate to your beliefs, your fears and your relationships, but any further comment would be irresponsible. I feel strongly that if you experience any further nightmares of this type then you should seek professional counselling to help you work through it.

I have had several nightmares of our youngest daughter drowning. These dreams can be very colourful and haunt me all day. Thank you if you can help.

Try to reach for the reason why you would think about your daughter drowning. Is she very young? Is your pool close by, or perhaps a neighbour's pool? Is there adequate fencing? Why not have her learn to swim to alleviate your fears? Are you the one who is afraid of the water? Did you nearly drown when you were young? Often we transfer our fears onto the next generation without knowing it. Emotion is represented by water and this dream may simply indicate that your daughter is growing up and this triggers a foreboding of loss.

6
The body and health

Dreams often warn us of impending health problems. These are known as *prodromic* dreams. The symbols appearing in them are usually graphic and leave the dreamer with a strong sense of foreboding on awakening.

From antiquity, the ability of dreams to predict and even to cure physical ailments was acknowledged. In classical Greece, dream incubation was a commonly employed method of healing (see page 19). In temples called Asklepia, dedicated to the God of Healing, Asklepios, the supplicant patient underwent a long purifying ritual involving bathing, sacrifice and dreaming. In the sacred precincts of the temple (which was peopled by snakes — long associated with both healing and rebirth)

[D]reams may have an anticipatory or prognostic aspect, and anybody trying to interpret them must take this into consideration, especially where an obviously meaningful dream does not provide a context sufficient to explain it ...

– C.G. Jung, *Man and His Symbols*

the patient took a sleeping draught and was left to sleep. Asklepios would appear in a dream, bringing a healing message. The dream was not interpreted; it was itself regarded as the cure.

Aristotle observed that it was highly probable that illness may be observed in dreams before manifesting because dreams had diagnostic powers. The Hippocratic treatises state that 'accurate knowledge of the signs which occur in dreams will be very valuable for all purposes'.

Freud surmised that the reason for this was that 'during sleep the mind, being diverted from the external world, is able to pay more attention to the interior of the body' (1958, p. 98). He also pointed out that the theory preferred by the medical establishment of his time for the origins of dreams was that the major function of dreams was to indicate impending physical problems.

Freud (1958, p. 97) noted that anxiety nightmares, culminating in a sudden, terrifying awakening, are often prevalent in dreamers with diseases of the heart; while those with lung disease are prone to dreams of suffocation, crowding or fleeing.

I have noted other common themes in dreamers who develop health problems. The car is a motif that often represents the physical body. If you are experiencing dreams about a car, then take note of the context. Are the brakes failing? Do you have to push it? Is it in control? All these themes are clues to the state of your physical health.

The house is another symbol often used by the dreaming mind to represent the physical self. Houses on fire can often point to ulcers or indigestion. One middle-aged woman related to me an occasionally recurring dream in which she pictured her ideal house in a state of disrepair. She said that she knew that whenever she experienced this dream it was a signal that she had been neglecting her health and that she needed more rest and an improved diet.

Dreams of being shot through the chest or crushed can often point to problems with the cardiovascular system or the lungs.

The distinguishing characteristic of health-related dreams is that they leave the dreamer with a strong physical sensation on awakening, not just a feeling. They may also be quite persistent, even if they do not recur with exactly the same images. If you are experiencing dreams of this nature, and suspect that they have a physical correlative, a visit to the doctor is definitely

In my dream I dreamt that I was nailed to a cross with only my palms and when I woke up my palms were sore.

Our hands symbolise protection, strength and authority, and sensing the pain after your dream, depicts a form of suffering even to the extent of self-punishment. What may be going on in your life now is that you feel you are losing your power. You may be the sort of person who always has a cross to bear. Do you suffer from arthritis or skin complaints concentrated around the hands or arms?

in order. However, for the main part, health dreams will simply be indications, like other dreams, that some rebalancing needs to be done in your life — in this case, lifestyle improved, stress reduced, a holiday taken.

My fiancé and my sister were walking with me in my dream beside a rocky fish-pond where there were large, white, flat fish swimming on the surface. My sister told us that these fish were deadly poisonous. As I walked on the rocks, I slipped into the pond, sinking deeper and deeper, and I couldn't swim upward. Looking up, I could see my sister and my fiancé looking down for me. The fish turned into skulls and I knew I was going to drown. I was suffocating and could feel myself choking underwater. I panicked, then consoled myself with the knowledge that my fiancé would die shortly anyway and we would be together.

(The day after this dream, the dreamer found a lump in her breast. It turned out to be benign. Immediately afterwards she experienced problems with her throat and at the time of writing was awaiting results of a blood test for problems with her thyroid.)

The fish is usually regarded as sacred, allied to the basic life force. Poisonous fish are not a good sign.

The strong sensation of being physically overwhelmed and unable to rise is the key here.

I was sitting in a cave which was greyish in colour and had a grey shawl around my head and body. Looking out, I saw white shapes moving very quickly and busily. These shapes reminded me of people I knew but they did not stop to acknowledge me. Then a person whom I have known for some time but not that well stood infront of me and said, 'There is something in your life that you have to change, and then you will get well'. He was about to leave when I grabbed hold of his finger and clung to it. He said gently, 'Don't get too emotional about us', and left.

(This dreamer had been off work for 3 months on sick leave and had just been diagnosed as having Chronic Fatigue Syndrome. She cringes at being asked to do anything on a regular, routine basis. When she was 3 weeks into her sickness she wondered why she wasn't recovering. She has been advised by doctors to have 3 to 6 months off work.)

Being clothed in grey in your dream symbolises your state of depression, inertia and indifference. These meanings are derived from the colour of ashes. But you can, like the phoenix, rise from the ashes if you rearrange your attitude to work and your life. That is the message of your little-known friend, who is also giving you a message about the state of your emotions. How have your emotions affected your situation? You can see the world going busily on outside, in white, which is the colour of purity, and also of medical settings, which you may have experienced a fair bit of lately.

I keep having a recurring dream that my bladder is full and I am dying to go to the toilet. But when I do, people are around me and I am embarrassed. I do go even with them there, but when I do I can't stop urinating.

(After seeking medical advice the dreamer was diagnosed as having thrush.)

The message is recurring in order that you take note of it. Going to the toilet often symbolises someone with pent-up emotions needing to let them out, but not able to because of repression or embarrassment. Thrush is often connected to emotional states also. The dream is indicating that you need to pay close attention to your urinary tract.

I dreamt I was working as a registered nurse in a nursing home, which is my work in real life, and that I was frantically running behind schedule. I happened to go to a long, enclosed verandah, and I saw a large, brown lump in what looked to be a pool of blood. When I looked more closely I saw it was a newborn foal. I couldn't see the mare that had given birth to it, so I fetched a teat and fed it. I looked again, and an elderly woman with grey hair appeared and I knew she had given birth to the foal. She looked deathly ill and pale. She pointed at me and said, 'Yours'. I asked if she meant that the foal belonged to me and she said, 'Yes'. Then she died. Thoughts of how I was going to care for the creature passed through my mind but in my heart I knew I wanted to keep it.

(The dreamer had not been working for a period of about 5 years when this dream occurred and was coming to the end of 7 years of awful stress which resulted in severe emotional and physical illness.)

Your dream represents that the period of difficulty is over. You are still a caring and thoughtful person. I would say that you should concentrate on achieving through other sources. You are probably someone who loses energy by sacrificing yourself for others. Care for yourself and for what is yours.

When my brother was 16 years old he had a dream that he was going to die of a heart attack by the time he reached 32. He didn't think much of it at the time, but some time later the dream recurred and has been coming to him on and off ever since. At the age of 25 years he had a mild heart attack. Is this dream a true prediction for the future?

His dream was certainly one that he did take notice of at the age of 16, and I suggest that, as he has already suffered from a mild heart attack, he keeps in extremely close contact with his doctors and that he definitely tells his doctors about his dreams. There are stronger precautions and medications being discovered constantly in the medical world for heart conditions. Yes, obviously, your brother's dream was a message preparing him to take care.

7

How to recall and interpret your dreams

Being able to interpret your own dreams will increase your awareness of the messages being conveyed and thus add

The interpretation of dreams and symbols demands intelligence ... Even a man of high intellect can go badly astray for lack of intuition or feeling.

– C.G. JUNG, *MAN AND HIS SYMBOLS*

an extra dimension to your life. I have devised a very simple system which, if followed routinely, will increase your dream recall and comprehension. It doesn't take long; it demands only readiness, interest and a little bit of commitment.

For those who have difficulty remembering dreams, you will find that the simple mind-set of *wanting* to remember, and actively taking steps to do so, will improve your recall dramatically. Some people have very strong dream memory; others do not. Ultimately, your success in recalling dreams will depend to a large extent on desire and application. Otherwise, the only dreams you will remember will be the unpleasant stuff of nightmares, which wake most of us from time to time.

The first and most important step is to buy a large, attractive notebook, with enough space on the page for diagrams, sketches, and text. Keep the notebook and writing instruments by your bed, within easy reach. Remember that this is a journal you keep for yourself: it is not for anyone else to read or examine, so you can feel comfortable with whatever you record. Like any other exercise that you do for yourself — eating well or keeping fit, for example — keeping your dream journal demand a certain commitment that is purely self-motivated, but has benefits that go well beyond the routine.

I suggest you use at least two pages for each day. In this way, you can record against the left page, for example, all the details you remember from your dreams, and break them down into themes. You should also note down the important events and preoccupations of the preceding day that you can remember. On the opposite page you can note feelings and possible meanings and your research on certain symbols. You may also wish to include sketches. Date every entry.

I strongly suggest that you go through your notebook before you begin and create headings and spaces to fill in as you proceed, following the method I will outline. This is a good idea because it means that as you wake up and turn each page, the journal has already been marked up. All you need to do is to recall and expand on the dream or dreams of the night. As we all know, dreams are, by nature, elusive in daylight hours. It is essential to minimise any thoughts or actions that may interpose between waking and recording your dream activity. If you have your notebook at the ready, and your pages already set up, then you are less likely to be distracted.

The other essential is time. It may be necessary to wake yourself 10 minutes earlier each morning, so that you are not rushed into the activities of the day. Regard it as your 10 minutes of creativity. Personally, I find it is much easier and more relaxing than running around the block first thing in the morning!

Don't be discouraged if your dream entries are incomplete or fragmented. You may find that you recall some passages and images very clearly, and forget others, or remember them only vaguely. Some days you may find it very hard to recall anything of note. Still, write it down and follow the steps. In this way, you will 'train' your memory to serve you more efficiently. Some dreamers have also reported to me that it helps if they concentrate their minds *before* going to sleep, by stating to themselves that they will dream during the night and that they will remember the dreams on waking. All of this preparation alerts the mind, and makes it more receptive. It establishes a conscious *intent*. The unconscious, which wants to be heard anyway, will eventually comply with a rich reserve of dreams. Don't give up. It may take some time to develop the 'muscles' for this new regimen.

If you wake up in the middle of the night from a vivid dream, it is best to note it down *immediately*. You do not need to follow all the steps: they can be elaborated in the morning. But it is very important to write out the sequence of the dream, otherwise you will find that it is much less clear on waking and you may have lost key images. This is another reason for having your dream journal within easy reach. It also helps to have a small bed-light (the less intrusive the better if you sleep with a partner). Once again, the aim is to record as much as possible without breaking your concentration.

Some writers on dreams have suggested that those whose dreams remain recalcitrantly vague wake themselves with an alarm during the middle of REM sleep. I think this is intrusive and unnecessary. If a dream wakes you out of REM sleep, it is by nature important (hence the necessity of having the journal close by); but to deliberately disrupt your sleep seems to me to be taking things too far.

THE FIVE STEPS

STEP ONE: RECORD YOUR DREAM

Write down your dream, in any form you wish, without being too concerned about syntax or sequence. The important thing to do is to get down on paper all the salient points you can remember. As you go, note anything that immediately comes to mind as the images unfold. It is especially important to note any strong feelings you have experienced in the dream. Don't spend too long on this, just write quickly and try to remember as much as you possibly can. A close examination will come later.

Equally, don't attempt to impose a structure. One of the characteristics of dreams is their looseness in structure, their sliding through time, place and personages. This poses a problem for our linear, conscious memory, and the usual purposes for which we record things on paper. If you are having particular difficulty with this, try imagining the dream as a movie. Draw sketches or diagrams if you find that it helps. Remember, the code is yours and yours alone; it needs to make sense only to you. Your dream journal is not an essay, an assignment or a report to the boss.

As you write and sketch, you will probably start to see the key elements of the dream come into focus.

Step Two: Examine your dream

Now it is time to look more closely at the dream. At this stage, I like to break the dream into segments for closer examination. First, note down the image or images that are strongest. You may simply want to underline them in the text of what you have already written. Note any strong colours. Is this a recurring dream or are there familiar images that appear in it? If this is the case, have they changed since the last dream of this nature?

Now, make entries under each of these four headings: Major themes, People and animals, Objects, Activity. You may not have something for every heading. For example, under Major themes you may write 'being chased, lost, missed train, flying over mountains'. It may be one theme, or several. For People and animals you may write 'the Queen, stroking my cat, chased by a bull, dog barking, man in black coat'. For Objects you may write 'lost wedding ring, antique furniture in room, cookies on plate, coffin'. For Activity, ask yourself where you were participating in the dream and where you were passive. Were the activities strenuous? Did you feel helpless?

There will be crossover to a certain extent with these entries, but do not regard this as a problem. The point of this part of the exercise is simply to highlight in some detail the major points of the dream. Don't get too hung up on rigorously matching segments. The system should serve to elucidate the dream, not dictate a structure.

The next stage is to write down beside your key elements any associations you have with them. Be strict with yourself here — only write down those associations that really mean something to you. If you have no specific associations for any of the symbols, but they seem to be particularly important in the context of the dream, then just note them with a question mark. These elements or images need further thought and research.

STEP THREE: NOTE YOUR FEELINGS

This is a very important step — possibly the most important — because it holds the key

to all the images and sequences of your dream. Underline or re-note all the feelings you have recorded in the text of your dream. Write down the feeling you had on waking. Next to all the images and themes you have written, note the feelings you had *in the dream*. The feelings may be completely different from those you would have towards the same object, person or event in the light of day. For example, you may have dreamt of being surrounded by spiders, and felt in the dream quite neutral or even positive about this, whereas if you had been in reality surrounded by spiders you probably would not have liked it one bit! You may find that, in recording your feelings, you discover further associations that you had not thought of before. Record these as well.

STEP FOUR: NOTE PREVIOUS DAY'S EVENTS

Note briefly the occurrences of the previous day: who you met; your concerns, anxieties and activities; any unusual sights that struck you; and your preoccupations. You may already have identified the key events of the previous day while going through the first three steps. If not, try to match any trigger events or thoughts with the images of your dream. If the hook still remains unclear, you may have to look back at preceding days, or themes that have been predominant in your recent life.

STEP FIVE: SYNOPSIS

By this stage of the process you may have achieved a sense of what your dream is about: you will have interpreted the symbols and images in conjunction with your feelings and the recent events of your waking life. At this stage, it is useful to go over all the data and make some notes about the nature of the issues raised by the dream, or the questions it poses you. Again, this can be written in any form you like: notes, sentences, even paragraphs if you have time.

In rare cases we have dreams that are not accessible, even when following the steps laid out above. Such dreams may be anticipatory; that is, they look forward to situations about to happen. If we are vigilant, life will present us with some very clear patterns; when we do not have time to be vigilant, it is our dreams that try to make us aware. If you have a dream that is still mystifying you after analysing it with the five steps, do not worry. Put it in the back of your mind and you may find that certain symbols fall into place over the next few days.

Archetypal dreams are another type of experience that may resist the standard analysis. These dreams are usually both more powerful and more ephemeral: powerful in the sense that they are especially striking; ephemeral in the sense that they hold meanings that transcend the nature of the everyday preoccupations with which you are concerned. These dreams tap into the broader rhythms of your life. So, while you may be able to identify certain elements that catch the hooks of your waking experience, the final meaning may be elusive, or may be comprehended only intuitively.

Some dreams are particularly interesting for the symbols and sequences they

present. After your brief interpretation, you may want to do some research into myths and symbols to enrich your understanding. Remember: dreams are multilayered. They are inevitably connected to your own life, but they may lead you down new paths of thought and possibility. It is up to you how far you want to take it!

SAMPLE DREAM RECORDS

Below are some sample dream records on a variety of themes. They follow the 5-step process I've just outlined. You may wish to refer to them to help you get started on your own dream analysis.

EXAMPLE 1: MIXING WITH ROYALTY

1. RECORD YOUR DREAM: Similar dreams over the past fortnight: first ones with me in the company of Princess Diana and Prince Charles, then the Duke and Duchess of York. Then I was at an important function where Queen Elizabeth and I were chatting, then she took me into the function room, and took me by the hands when the national anthem was played. Last night I dreamt I was with Priscilla Presley and a childhood friend on a cruise and we became close friends. Always in colour. Very enjoyable.

2. **EXAMINE YOUR DREAM**: Intimacy with members of the Royal Family; childhood friend; being friends with movie star; colour.

3. **NOTE YOUR FEELINGS**: Satisfaction and happiness.

4. **NOTE PREVIOUS DAY'S EVENTS**: Reading, relaxing; being on holiday; a neighbour dropped by; ordinary household chores.

5. **SYNOPSIS**: A really pleasant dream. My everyday life: the dream is reinforcing my sense of contentment. Not intimidated by people who lead more elevated lives: feel as if I can tap into that in my dreams, where I can enjoy anyone's company! The colour reinforces the sense of pleasure.

EXAMPLE 2 : BEING AT WAR

1. **RECORD YOUR DREAM**: Dream about being in a war: always on the run in trench warfare on the beach. Running through minefields with a brightly lit rainbow

shining over the battlefield. Come through it all without a scratch on me.

2. **Examine your dream:** Running; beach; warfare everywhere; running through minefields; rainbow; not hurt.

3. **Note your feelings:** Need to survive; unsafe; certain sense of confidence that I will get through.

4. **Note previous day's events:** Had doctor's appointment which gave good prognosis; appointments to do with work; found it difficult to get to sleep.

5. **Synopsis:** Haven't been feeling well lately: relieved after today's check-up to find that doctor has found the beginnings of an ulcer: we had thought there was a possibility of cancer. Rainbow over battlefield is a good omen, probably reflecting my sense of relief. The war is the stress I've been under personally and at work. Need to reflect on rainbow and not on trenches.

Example 3: The vampires

1. **Record your dream:** Dream in which large organisation of vampires from around

the country wanted to kill me. Didn't know reason why. I was in a car with a girl that I knew in the dream (but not in real life) and her grandmother. The girl was not a vampire but her grandmother was and wanted to kill me. I had the girl stop the car and I got out, saying I was going to a house which I claimed was where I lived. But this was a trick to convince her grandmother to go to the wrong house when she came to kill me. I went into the house and the owner let me in. As soon as the girl and her grandmother had driven away I left and went down the block to another house, which I entered. However, the couple that lived there were vampires and I left again. They did not come after me. Then went down the street again and into a house where four males were playing music as they had a rock band. I felt protected with them and spent time feeling happy and safe.

2. **Examine your dream:** Vampires; girl; grandmother; car; houses; couple; four males; being searched for and threatened; unable to find safe place.

3. **Note your feelings:** Feeling threatened; feeling unsafe; not knowing where the vampires would find me; having to

trick them; searching for a place to hide; feeling safe in the end.

4. NOTE PREVIOUS DAY'S EVENTS: Had another argument with my family over simply nothing. They don't believe I can do anything without asking for their approval. I had a coffee with my best friend and her friend asked me if I wanted to flat with her.

5. SYNOPSIS: Was offered a home away from home today; felt sucked dry of energies by my family (I think this was the grandmother figure in the dream). I think the girl was a part of me, the car my ride through life. I had to get out of the car because it was not safe. Time to move in a different way in life. My distrust of people's motives and what they want from me comes out. Sometimes I 'trick' people by changing the topic or by avoidance to stop them focusing on my real feelings. I feel more comfortable with men than women, particularly in the family. I feel safe with creative men.

EXAMPLE 4: SUICIDE

1. RECORD YOUR DREAM: I am happily doing things around the house, then suddenly I am in my bedroom. It is dark and there is a chair and a rope hanging from the ceiling and tied around my neck. I am standing on the chair and every time I lift my foot I seem to be falling. I wake and find myself actually standing on a chair (there is no rope, of course) and gasping for air. I am worried on awaking.

2. **EXAMINE YOUR DREAM**: Change from doing happy things to something more morbid; bedroom; the dark; a chair and a rope; ceiling; falling.

3. **NOTE YOUR FEELINGS**: Indifference; alarm on awaking.

4. **NOTE PREVIOUS DAY'S EVENTS**: Usual routine, studied with my teacher and a few others after school; drove around with a few friends; played some pool at the pub; came home and went to my room to study some more.

5. **SYNOPSIS**: I think the bedroom is a private part of myself where my deepest thoughts are hidden. Why do I want to hang myself? Is life so bad? I've had this dream frequently over the past 2 months, which means the message is strong. Perhaps the feeling of falling reflects my fear of

falling down in someone's estimation, or my fear of not doing well in my exams. I haven't been feeling well lately, and I think I should get a medical check-up.

EXAMPLE 5: SPIDERS

1. RECORD YOUR DREAM: I have dreamt about red-back spiders. When I killed them in my dream, they sprayed back onto me thousands of little baby spiders who attack me. I am very upset on waking.

2. EXAMINE YOUR DREAM: Red and black; spiders; attack and fear of death.

3. NOTE YOUR FEELINGS: Feeling very threatened and scared; upset on waking.

4. NOTE PREVIOUS DAY'S EVENTS: Family and daughter cross because I live alone; felt insecure all day; talked to a friend who is a widow, too, and shared private thoughts.

5. SYNOPSIS: Somehow, the spider seems to represent my feelings of fear and aloneness. Living alone without my husband has affected my self-esteem. Perhaps there are spiders around me? I should check. The red-back is deadly. I was overwhelmed by them.

I should make sure that my house is secure. I think I need to throw off the feelings of too many worries or problems.

EXAMPLE 6: THE EX-LOVER

1. RECORD YOUR DREAM: I am walking with my ex-boyfriend (we are very good friends) and we both end up in a building which may or may not be an apartment building. A man suddenly appears who stabs me repeatedly with his knife. There is blood everywhere. I can feel the knife going in.

2. EXAMINE YOUR DREAM: Ex-boyfriend; building; man; knife; blood.

3. NOTE YOUR FEELINGS: Scared; slightly puzzled.

4. NOTE PREVIOUS DAY'S EVENTS: Met my new boyfriend for lunch; my ex-boyfriend rang me in the afternoon at work; cooked dinner for myself and watched television.

5. SYNOPSIS: I think I am holding onto my feelings for my ex-boyfriend. I think this dream signifies that I should let go of these fantasies.

EXAMPLE 7: TIDAL WAVE

1. RECORD YOUR DREAM: Had recurring dream which happens occasionally. It is a nightmare. I am standing at a shoreline and a wall of water emerges, higher than any building I can imagine. I feel I cannot breathe. I have someone with me — it is my little girl, the youngest. We reach the safety of a building with strong windows where we watch the terrible force of the wave break. Sometimes there are sharks surfing the wave.

2. EXAMINE YOUR DREAM: Daughter; wall of water; terror; strong windows keeping out the water; sharks.

3. NOTE YOUR FEELINGS: Overwhelming fear.

4. NOTE PREVIOUS DAY'S EVENTS: Nothing spectacular — an ordinary day. I didn't answer my husband back when I really didn't agree with what he had told the children. My mother wanted me to help her do some shopping. The children had to be picked up from school and taken to their dancing and sport lessons. I felt tired all day.

5. **SYNOPSIS:** I know that waves and water represent emotions, and I think that I am feeling overwhelmed at the moment. My daughter in the dream reminds me of me as a small child. This feeling of being at breaking point emotionally has been with me for many years. My more sensitive self is often hurt by those around me. I don't speak out enough. As a younger person I was more accepting of this, but now I cannot stand and watch myself being affected by and almost drowning in my feelings that are not recognised by others. I think it is time I spoke up for myself. The sharks are probably representing threatening people.

Sweet dreams

It is my greatest wish for you, the dreamer, to gain an insight into your creative, adventurous inner self (which you may not think you have) by way of your dreams. I have been able to enrich my life with my own dreams and with the dreams of others. You can, too, but only if you have the determination to go out and investigate your 'other' self.

Pay as much attention to your dream life as you would your love life or even your sex life! Take the time to reminisce and contemplate the dream images that belong only to you. Don't be afraid to look back, because by doing so your intuition and your instinctive dreams will help you face the future.

I urge you to wake up to your dreams and discover the hidden treasures that your mind — your subconscious mind — is ready to share with you.

Sweet dreams always!

References

Campbell, Joseph 1959, *Primitive Mythology: The Masks of God,* Penguin, New York.

Freud, Sigmund [1958] 1991, *The Interpretation of Dreams,* Penguin, London.

Hawley, Janet 1995, 'The Hero's Journey', *Good Weekend Magazine,* 14 October.

Jung, C. G. 1978, *Man and His Symbols,* Picador, London.

Jung, C. G. 1985, *Dreams,* Ark, London.

Jung, C. G. 1993, *Memories, Dreams, Reflections,* recorded and edited by Aniela Jaffe, Fontana Press, London.

LaBerge, Stephen & Rheingold, Howard 1990, *Exploring the World of Lucid Dreaming,* Ballantine, New York.

Lawlor, Robert 1991, *Voices of the First Day,* Millennium, Newtown, New South Wales.

Storr, Anthony 1983, *The Essential Jung,* Princeton University Press, New Jersey.

Index